Individual Motivation

Individual Motivation
Removing the Blocks to Creative Involvement

Étienne Minarik

Publisher's Message by
Norman Bodek, President
Productivity, Inc.

Productivity Press, Inc.

CAMBRIDGE, MASSACHUSETTS

NORWALK, CONNECTICUT

Productivity Press, Inc.
P.O. Box 3007
Cambridge, MA 02140
Telephone: (617) 497-5146
Telefax: (617) 868-3524

Cover design by Joyce C. Weston
Printed and bound by Maple-Vail Book Manufacturing Group
Printed in the United States of America on acid-free paper

Library of Congress Cataloging-in-Publication Data

Minarik, Etienne.
    [Motivation individuelle, clé du succès de l'entreprise. English.]
    Individual motivation : removing the blocks to creative involvement / Etienne Minarik.
        p. cm.
    Translation of: Motivation individuelle, clé du succès de l'entreprise.
    Includes index.
    ISBN 0-915299-85-2
    1. Employee motivation.   2. Work groups.   3. Organizational change.
I. Title.
HF5549.5.M63M56   1992
658.3'14--dc20   91-28947
                                                             CIP

92 93 94 10 9 8 7 6 5 4 3 2 1

Contents

Activities Spill Over into Operational Functions
Activities Spill Over into Management Functions
Harmony among Various Types of Motivation

Publisher's Message

Continuing our tradition as a publisher of significant books with a global perspective on manufacturing management, we are pleased to introduce the work of Étienne Minarik, a Hungarian-born expert on the organization of work who has more than 20 years' experience in guiding the change process for a number of major French companies. Minarik's book, *Individual Motivation*, has a simple, powerful message: the key to competitive advantage in a saturated market is the effective use of a company's human resources.

Most manufacturing work is compartmentalized vertically and horizontally, the legacy of a system that worked well in an unsaturated market where high volume was king. Although the front lines performing the work today often know the most about product and process, they tend to lack information and decision-making power, reserved for upper levels of the hierarchy. On a horizontal level, their role is limited to production; associated functions such as administrative or maintenance support are delegated to other departments. These limitations are the source of negative expressions, and of attempts to placate them through benefits, labor action, and similar remedies.

As this timely book shows, today's competitive market requires a flexibility that compartmentalized organizations cannot provide. *Individual Motivation* demonstrates how individual initiative can take root and flower in an empowered environment, allowing a company to better meet the changing needs of its customers.

In the United States and many other countries, a combination of economic and human necessity is driving corporate managers to rethink traditional approaches to the organization of work. The employee involvement movement is evolving into a new management structure in many companies, based on self-directed work teams that deal with many functions once exclusively handled by managers or specialists.

Self-directed teams have come about to fill a need for a work structure that respects and utilizes the intelligence and abilities of the people closest to the job or to the customer. Consistent with the same purpose, Minarik gives us a fresh perspective on the motivational side of work organization and shows how even a lone innovative manager can start to bring about change in an old-style company culture. *Individual Motivation* proposes a strategy that motivates and fulfills the employees as it creates the flexibility to meet changing market demands. It is a daring, bottom-up approach, but one that any committed manager can learn to follow.

Minarik presents his approach through a case study involving machine shop foreman Raymond Dupont, a composite character drawn from the author's extensive consulting experience. As we follow Dupont's dealings with his work group, we see situations and attitudes that are not so different from what we could see in any other Western factory. France is certainly not the only place where companies struggle to contain costs and remain competitive, where factories suffer from absenteeism, where piecework employees turn to hobbies and other non-work interests for their real fulfillment, or where labor representatives bypass knowledgeable supervisors to deal with upper management.

Dupont, a bright, observant person, realizes that this is a sorry state for the company to be in and muses on what to do about it. He begins talking with his workers — and listening to what they say to him. Gradually, he earns their trust and, without asking authority from his superiors, he starts to experiment with the work structure in the group.

One of his first changes involves two workers who had obligations that took each off the job for parts of some days. Rather than disciplining them for absenteeism, Dupont listens to their situation and takes a radical approach: he assigns them to work together as a tandem, measuring their output jointly instead of individually. The two workers become much more productive in this arrangement, and their supervisor's concern changes their attitudes toward the job.

Seeing the positive results from this tandem effort, Dupont institutes other shared output arrangements among the team members, then goes further. Observing the various abilities in his machine shop group, he begins to find assignments for people that suit their individual interests and aptitudes. Dupont discovers that aspects for which certain workers had been criticized can be turned to advantage for the team. One worker, for example, was considered slow, but in fact he was quite conscientious about what he did. Although his output was low, he could approach and solve technical problems that others could not. With the group output collectively increased, Dupont is able to assign this worker difficult tasks that frustrate the others. As a result, the worker shows his capabilities and becomes a respected member of the team.

Slowly, Dupont rearranges his team's internal structure, creating a skill team that matches individual aptitudes with various jobs. The team dramatically reduces its costs and productivity steadily increases, but it is still somewhat stifled. Many of the functions that directly affect the team's work lie outside the team structure, either higher up the management chain, or horizontally organized into a functional department. As Dupont's experiment becomes more widely known around the plant, he puts together a skill group of the supervisors of various horizontal departments, who assist each other and coordinate their employees' activities. Ultimately, upper management recognizes the benefits of the arrangement Dupont has informally created and reorganizes the plant with a flattened hierarchy that moves decision-making authority closer to the work.

Individual Motivation is inspiring in its assertion that organizational change can be driven successfully at the front-line levels. From this story of individual transformations and calculated personal risks, a set of principles emerges to guide the process of change in manufacturing organizations.

Through the story of Raymond Dupont, managers can experience an approach for organizational change that shows how employees' "negative individualism" — often manifested as frustrated behavior or indifference — can be transformed into innate creativity and initiative.

From the experience of Raymond Dupont, *Individual Motivation* extracts a model that managers can use to begin to shape manufacturing work around the unique aptitudes of the people who perform it. Using this approach, a manager can begin to turn employees' personal characteristics into assets, skillfully integrating them in a responsive team-based approach. As the work becomes more satisfying for employees, you can count on them for creative responses that solve problems and fulfill customer needs. The bottom-line results are lower costs and increased productivity — outcomes that serve everyone in the company.

We would like to express our appreciation to a number of people who were involved in the preparation of the English edition of *Individual Motivation*. We thank Étienne Minarik for writing the book and answering our translation questions. Our appreciation goes to Monique Engrand of Les Editions d'Organisation for permitting us to publish this edition, and also to Martine Bassett for her assistance with translation matters.

A word of thanks to Productivity Press general manager Steven Ott for sponsoring the publication of this book in English. Karen Jones was the developmental editor for the project, with translation assistance from Bruce Graham; Dorothy Lohmann managed the manuscript preparation, with assistance from Rosemary Winfield, copyeditor, and Jennifer Cross, proofreader; David Lennon managed book production, with typesetting and graphics by Gayle Joyce and Michele Saar. The cover was designed by Joyce C. Weston.

Norman Bodek
President
Productivity, Inc.

Preface

"A medium-sized company with just four hundred employees locates in the United States or Japan and competes with giant companies that were unbeatable just a decade ago."

This kind of news is no longer rare. In fact, it is becoming typical in a competitive market economy where the criteria for growth are quick reactions, constant innovation, and heavy staff input — not simply size.

In these often-dramatic success stories, employees work practically unsupervised, with broad responsibility, in a system free of constraints. They solve most practical problems and cope effectively with the many disturbances inherent in competition.

Such varied and efficient input is possible because the tasks have been regrouped and distributed — not according to the old principle of job specialization but rather according to each individual employee's best aptitudes. The individual is not arbitrarily subjected to the constraints of a particular organization of work; instead, the organization adapts to the individual. The result is harmonious reciprocity.

Rapid technological advances have computerized management and information networks, making many middle managers unnecessary and facilitating the development of an individualized organization that actively solicits employees' contributions.

This fast and flexible new operational structure often yields impressive results. Work teams in large factories can function with the flexibility of a small business. They can successfully pay off their operating expenses almost day to day. They operate with practically no inventory of merchandise or raw materials, so they avoid debt and interest charges. By drawing fully on their employees' "creative individualism," these small business units gain a comfortable technical and economic advantage over their competitors. Even though in many firms such individualism is traditionally negative and causes more losses than gains, these firms transform it into a source of innovation and creativity.

How is it possible to unblock initiative? How can we make individualism creative? Are there tricks or easy formulas for obtaining this valuable increased input? Can models be applied uniformly?

One characteristic of competitive economies in developed countries is that the conditions for each facility in the manufacturing and service industries become specific to a particular business niche — the equipment, products, nature of the competition, and market demands. In the past, the same organizational model was effective everywhere; today each facility must develop its own model and must unblock initiative according to its own constraints. Although large-scale trends definitely do exist, they may manifest themselves differently in each instance.

This brings us to the main subject of this book, which both identifies the need to unblock initiative (Part One) and describes the particular conditions in one large company (Part Two) that successfully implemented this new idea and fostered strong input from its employees. This approach is thus not a formula or model, but rather an example — an experience that invites further thought and analysis.

Government agencies, labor unions, or research institutes cannot assume responsibility for unblocking initiative in businesses. They can definitely provide assistance to all types of firms, but they clearly cannot achieve this essential change for them.

Government cannot go much further than repealing antiquated regulations and facilitating the accumulation of investment capital through tax incentives. Despite their different political systems, governments in certain central European countries currently subject to the same competitive mechanisms as Western Europe are increasingly withdrawing from direct management of companies in order to unleash the creative energies of workers. It is not the political system but rather the unblocking of personal initiative that increases economic efficiency.

Despite market demands, however, change is often slow: habits, tradition, and resistance present formidable opposition. Scarcely a decade ago, boards of directors and even general managers performed an operational role. Now they must apply themselves to the tasks of development, strategy, and future projections. Before the crisis,* responsibilities were centralized at the top levels of management, but now they must be transferred to the front lines of the organization to increase the speed of problem solving. Before the economic shift, departments and production units were enveloped by various constraints that required employees to spend their time doing simple, repetitive tasks. In today's economy we must unshackle jobs, unblock initiative, and harness creative individualism.

---

* The crisis in Western Europe (1974-1982) was similar to the crisis faced in the United States in the early 1980s. It was a period of adapting enterprises to automation and computer technologies, accompanied by increasing competition and also by layoffs and unemployment. — Ed.

Compartmentalized tasks — the result of excessive, and at one time necessary, specialization — are now rapidly being replaced by automation. Other tasks change in nature. Although productivity gains initially demand considerable investment, they later require only organizational and structural reform. In fact, the gains achieved are so substantial that they offset the difference between the high employee benefit costs paid by Western employers and the much lower costs of their Asian competitors. These gains can even transform this difference into an advantage if the employees' input encounters no further obstacles.

Companies where such change progresses quickly come out ahead of the competition. But when a conservative attitude delays or prevents change, employee individualism is often a negative factor.

The initiative and perseverance of a machine shop foreman, Raymond Dupont,* in the experiment described in Part Two, resulted in enhanced awareness and rapid expansion of the experiment throughout his shop. Initiative was gradually unblocked throughout the plant, and the creative individualism of the employees became the fundamental operating principle for departments and production units.

---

* Raymond Dupont is a "typical" French name, the equivalent of "Bob Smith" in the United States. Dupont is a composite character, based on the author's consulting experience with a number of French manufacturing companies. He represents a whole class of foremen and middle managers who have a sense of reality and use it to bypass the impediments raised by the traditional operational structure to more effectively use the skills and abilities of their employees. — Ed.

PART ONE

Creative Individualism:
A Growth Factor

Introduction

The individualism and resourcefulness of the French are pervasive topics in French literature. Year after year, studies and anthologies sometimes tolerantly document and at other times harshly lampoon such individualism.

Average French men and women are portrayed as eternally unsatisfied people who gripe and grumble, criticize and quarrel. They would back away, it is said, if offered real responsibilities, or if shown the complexities of management and enterprise.

They may clamor for responsibility, but only because they know that they would refuse it if offered. They continue to gripe and grumble, in order to ease their conscience, but they are not deeply motivated to assume responsibility, according to political, management, and labor representatives.

Raymond Dupont, a machine shop foreman, conducted an experiment on this phenomenon. Dupont, an inquisitive and experienced man, was inclined to report his observations to his superiors. But he also had abilities that enabled him to implement his own suggestions in order to make his shop procedures very flexible. At that time, everyone worked on a piecework basis — a restrictive system that relied on external motivation, imposed discipline through the hierarchy, and was not very efficient.

Raymond Dupont wanted to change this system, and interest his workers in the affairs of their plant. Such changes required organizational reforms.

Dupont made a choice different from the one often described in lampoons and amusing anecdotes. Instead of becoming a grumbler, a malcontent, and a dissenter — and thus be deprived of resources and responsibilities — he decided to act. Not having the right to do so in the extremely hierarchical organization of his plant, he risked acting more or less illegally, in the interest of his workers and his company.

When his achievement was discovered, it became an example for the rest of the plant to follow. Through this foreman's perseverance, plant managers learned that a source of tremendous efficiency lay imprisoned by antiquated constraints. The intelligence and occupational know-how of department and shop personnel were being used only to perform individual procedures, even though employees were capable of observing dysfunctions, solving practical problems, and developing small innovations in order to contribute to the plant's economic success. Organizational tradition was so strong, however, that only customary resources were being used despite growing competition.

The originality of Dupont's approach was to release internal motivations and appeal to the creative individualism of his workers. He found a new means of productivity that was well suited to the demands of a difficult market.

But what exactly did he do? Just as the government tries to repeal old, outmoded laws, he did away with antiquated constraints — such as closely circumscribed jobs and the piecework system — that blocked initiative and stifled creative individualism.

He individualized team organization by substituting collective output for piecework constraints that were the symbols of large scale and specialization.Through this reform, he was able to distribute the work load according to new criteria — namely, personal experiences and aptitudes — while appearing to remain within the old qualification system and the piecework system.

Dupont began this endeavor because the barriers and constraints of a rigid organization caused significant *losses* — nearly one hour of work time per day per person lost, social tensions, structural compartmentalization and isolation, excessive union zeal and grievance-mongering, small hidden innovations, and an increase in negative individualism. A multitude of small losses contributed to this general downward trend. The financial consequences of this trend proved to be particularly dangerous after a rapid intensification of competition. High prices, burdened by unproductive costs of almost 20 percent, created a competitive disadvantage.

The foreman's actions reversed this downward trend on the local level: the team's costs dropped more than 15 percent and overall output improved.

Employees on the team worked on the basis of personal motivation. The team had good collective output and no need for the labor-management escape valve that other production units relied on.

Moreover, the new system could be expanded. Individualized organization allows responsibility for certain operational and organizational duties to be transferred to the team and the front lines. Increasingly upgraded equipment and computerization of decentralized, specialized, hierarchical data make it possible — and even necessary, in competitive conditions — to regroup responsibilities wherever practical problems arise. Aside from being more effective, this approach also builds strong additional motivation.

The experience of this team and its rapid replication in other sectors illustrate that human behavior is not inevitably and inalterably conservative — even within the context of a large company. If the environment encourages behavior to evolve, it *can* change in content and orientation. When sociopolitical conditions and the organizational conditions of businesses are favorable, behavior even can extend beyond current reality and affect the future. This is the source of inventions, innovations, and cooperative efforts among individuals and among different organizational functions.

CHAPTER ONE

Creative Individualism:
A Source of Motivation

An Old Story

The rigid organization that prevented Raymond Dupont's plant from adapting to a highly competitive market and propelled him to transform his team into a skill group has a long tradition.

Like so many others, the company began modestly, but a long period of heavy growth encouraged and stimulated its rapid expansion. In three decades, it had grown to 3,000 employees.

Before World War II, the plant's modest production units were organized according to the principle of job specialization. This practice had begun a century earlier and, just before World War I, was conceptualized into a theory of organization. The fundamental idea of extreme specialization of jobs and functions dominated management theory throughout most of the century.

At this plant, the application of this theory was simple, at least in the beginning: it isolated production jobs in the work process, and grouped them in production units. Small departments were created upstream and downstream from the production units. These departments took charge of the preparatory tasks that were needed for effective production but that, if integrated into the jobs, would impede the rhythm, continuity, and stability of the work. This was the turn-of-the-century organizational theory that had justified the breaking up of units into specialized operations.

The theory was not applied with the customary rigor in this plant. While the company remained small, the departments above and below production units remained in an embryonic state. Performance was supervised by a single line manager who reported to the president/founder. The line manager maintained direct contact with the workers. Working relations were cordial but within an authoritarian framework. People still knew each other well, and handymen often were used as emergency mechanics to avoid waiting for the small maintenance department to intervene.

In short, the plant had a rigid operational structure that applied the principle of specialization of jobs and functions, but direct relations between workers and managers significantly reduced the negative consequences of compartmentalized work.

The plant's rapid expansion upset this balance. In the context of an unsaturated market, orders increased sharply, and the plant grew larger each year to boost production. With this expansion, organizational flexibility was lost, and a stimulating environment disappeared.

The embryonic departments positioned above and below the production units expanded into full administrative departments that were given broad responsibilities. Production workers thus became completely compartmentalized, and lost their administrative responsibilities and finally their motivation. Productivity increased, but the deteriorating interpersonal atmosphere led to a significant increase in managerial staff. This dynamic stimulated the rapid evolution of the management hierarchy and the subsequent proliferation of levels of management.

Relationships that formerly were cordial and stimulating became restrictive and demotivating. Delimiting jobs horizontally within functional departments and vertically within the management hierarchy did not permit full utilization of personal potential and qualifications.

The plant's organization probably could have developed in some other way, but when a rigid operational structure is profitable and ensures considerable productivity, no one looks for an operational structure that reconciles personal aptitudes with productivity. Economic and social issues become increasingly dissociated from each other.

Nevertheless, the company attempted to do away with the drawbacks of a rigid organization through external methods of motivation. Wages were an incentive based on individual output. The various jobs were arranged in a complex classification system, while tasks (of which jobs were comprised) were organized hierarchically by a qualification system according to their number and degree of complexity. Transitions to better-paying jobs or to higher, more advantageous classifications were tied to strict criteria applied by the personnel office. But all of these incentive methods became new constraints, further reinforcing job specialization.

This dramatic increase in management and administrative powers and responsibilities led to an increase in the powers of organized labor and of the role played by union representatives of the employees.

In effect, labor representatives gained authority as workers grew increasingly frustrated by compartmentalized work. In some production units, their powers and responsibilities within the company went beyond the usual scope of the protective role and replaced the corporate chain of command. Even strictly occupational problems passed through this labor organization channel rather than the official hierarchy. This change in communication channels did not unblock anything, however, for jobs continued to be surrounded by demotivating constraints.

Toward the end of the period of intense growth, a sprawling organization had stripped production units of their autonomy and controlled them by divisions; the various preparatory phases for production, such as research, purchasing, and work assignment, were shared by several departments or services. In short, successive barriers were superimposed vertically and horizontally, fragmenting responsibilities into specialized parts.

Over the decades, the simple idea of specialization of jobs and functions was thus transformed into a huge, compartmentalized, rigid organization that erected demotivating barriers on all sides. Not until the rapid development of market competition in the mid-1970s did the serious drawbacks blocking personal initiative and motivation become apparent.

In fact, the computerization of management and data, and the emergence of a new generation of equipment capable of performing complete operations, renders extreme job specialization useless. Complex systems of superimposed structures appear rigid and conservative because they cannot adapt to the new technical and economic demands imposed by the competitive market: they lack the growth criteria of innovation, personal initiative, and intensive use of the creative individualism of employees in the lower levels of the organization.

Unblocking Organizations
Stimulates Creative Individualism

How can we stimulate personal initiative and unleash internal motivation? Attempts to unblock motivation have proliferated under the pressure of an increasingly competitive environment, and they have met with varying degrees of success.

Sometimes we simply reinforce old mechanisms. Instead of removing barriers, we create, for example, a coordinating body; instead of integrating quality control into production jobs, we create a rework unit. This approach usually produces "remedial" organizations.

When external methods of motivation are attempted without unblocking the jobs, progress can be made, but conflicts of interest can be created as well. Examples include suggestion boxes, special bonuses, training programs, employee discussion meetings, and quality circles.

In contrast, more advanced approaches dismantle the many obstructive mechanisms contained in a rigid operational structure and, on an experimental basis, replace the principle of specialization with the principle of job individualization. To reach this goal, large corporations turn their plants or offices into subsidiaries. Within large facilities, extensive autonomy is granted to production units to unblock jobs in these basic cells by removing old constraints and regrouping scattered functions wherever practical problems arise.

As outdated constraints disappear and certain administrative and management responsibilities are integrated into lower-level jobs, the nature of working relationships changes: relationships become reciprocal and stimulating.

Raymond Dupont oversaw this complex transformation (described in detail later) throughout the machining area after his experiment was proved successful. Because this program simplified the organizational structure and its overlapping functions, the labor organization channel was no longer the preferred way of resolving problems.

Individualizing jobs based on personal aptitudes is a difficult phase in the process of unblocking motivation. The principle of specialization must be abandoned, and one of adaptation of jobs to personal aptitude must be substituted. Compartmentalized functions must be regrouped at the lowest level in the organization, which often means restructuring management's perceptions of the abilities of supervisors and workers. In addition, mechanisms for evaluation and remuneration must be set up within working groups to reinforce the desire to generate innovations and assume initiative.

Such change upsets the established relationships and value systems within traditional organizational hierarchies. This situation clearly implies a major behavioral change.

The stakes are considerable. Indeed, employees' internal motivation today represents industry's surest guarantee of growth.

In an individualized organization, the barriers to and constraints on creative individualism are replaced by positions of responsibility that are individualized, but they also remain undefined and can be competed for by anyone who demonstrates the ability and qualifications to do the job.

Social Organization Determines Motivation

Competition is not what it used to be. Even tradition and social organization of countries now play an active role in it. External conditions determined by the social organization of each country also play a major role in developing a company's operational structure. These external conditions can facilitate or hinder efforts to foster employees' creative individualism.

In some industrialized countries, social organizations are motivational, and personal behavior is seen as representing national characteristics such as cooperation, discipline, responsibility, or innovation. These national characteristics have become an especially valuable success factor since the acceleration of economic change. Studies of the sources of personal motivation always discover reasons closely linked to national history, tradition, and social organization.

When governments traditionally have a high degree of administrative decentralization, an enhanced sense of responsibility and spirit of initiative are evident at the local level, in districts and regions. On the other hand, in traditions of political and administrative centralization, people tend to wait for action to be initiated from above. In the long run, such passive expectations may create negative and critical attitudes.

An educational system that teaches students to observe physical, economic, literary, social, and other phenomena develops experimental and inductive reasoning. In a theoretical system of instruction based on exposition and application of physical, economic, social, and other laws, students use deductive reasoning, which is not conducive to observation and experimentation. These two tendencies produce different outcomes, depending on the tradition and social organization of different countries. Although the economic consequences of these two motivational directions were not significant during the period of intense growth, their presence is being increasingly felt since the economic crisis.

Organization of Work Determines Motivation

What is true at the national level is also true within the smaller context of an individual company. In the same market segment or traditional business sector some organizations threatened by competition have not only succeeded in changing but have also expanded, while others have found it necessary to ask for government assistance.

The difference comes principally from the employees' efforts on the job. In the first case, the workers are motivated, and overall goals coincide with their aspirations, while in the second instance, the two are in opposition.

If worker motivation represents a decisive factor in success, then why do so many businesses and government agencies fail to use it? It is probably a question of will and know-how.

In many cases, habit is so strong that companies may attempt to replace effective motivation with other means such as computerization, automation, strengthening of management, or more elaborate job specialization, while forgetting that, in a new economic environment, these methods lose much of their former effectiveness.

In other instances, companies may encourage employee participation but without tampering with the customary operational structure, for fear of slipping up or rocking the boat. They may try to introduce motivation into the workplace externally, without tampering with the content or organization of jobs. Although training programs, meetings, and clubs can influence employee motivation, their influence is neither profound nor lasting.

Finally, businesses (and even the civil service in some countries) that understand that creating effective motivation requires them to adapt their operations to this new criterion for success begin revising the organization of departments and production units. Testing new mechanisms for overall change may take years, but it results in learning the art of organizational change and creating new operational structures for departments and production units, based on the criterion of employee motivation.

Market Imperatives Influence Organization

The last and most complex of the responses just described is the most promising one. But how is it possible to win this gamble, so that the work organization will adapt to the criterion of fuller utilization of personal potential and abilities? How can we ensure that the jobs themselves will generate this all-important creative motivation?

This book attempts to explore these issues not only on the theoretical level but also on the practical level, by describing in detail the difficulties and successes encountered by Raymond Dupont in his factory. First we must accurately define the relationship of motivation to various other success factors.

Until recently, motivation was hardly considered a decisive factor in corporate success. Although upper management acknowledged the need for motivating managers, other occupational categories, particularly the "doers," were not felt to either need or respond to motivation. This was equally true in the various segments of the service industries and in the manufacturing sector's production units and departments. In fact, the work organization most generally used during the period of intense growth had no need for workers to be internally motivated.

Why was this so? In the highly industrialized nations, the market did not show lasting signs of saturation until the end of the 1960s, due to rapid technological development that significantly increased technical production capacity. An unsaturated market requires mass production in large quantities, and when the technical level of production capacity is inadequate, the organization of work must compensate for the deficiency. This explains the rapid expansion of compartmentalized organization at the turn of the century: it was an operational structure based on the principle of specialization of jobs and functions.

In this type of organization, departments, jobs, and production units are expected to perform their own roles properly and not to be concerned about other functions. The kind of motivation that might succeed in this type of cellular, compartmentalized operation might come from satisfaction for a job well done or fondness for detail.

On the other hand, a desire to initiate, to think, to understand not only the part but the whole process as well does not fit within this operational structure. Antagonisms between personal abilities and organizational constraints are inherent in this situation.

But developing a desire to work in a certain way is not just a personal inclination passed on by genes. It is also a social, cultural, and educational phenomenon.

The sciences and education have made enormous progress since the turn of the century, but the skills and know-how they have developed are rarely used in the world of work. Nevertheless, they have documented new social and personal motivations, such as the desire to understand, initiate, and assume responsibility. These needs have been researched in business firms, banks, and hospitals, as well as in industrial companies.

But implementing these new social and personal motivations met with resistance from work organizations whose basic principle remained unchanged.

A growing antagonism, apparent even before World War II, led to interpersonal and social conflicts, intensified during the ensuing long period of intense economic growth. The antagonism was exacerbated by four variables:

- An unsaturated market,
- Insufficient technical capacity,
- Compartmentalized work, and
- Externally imposed motivation.

This is the classic situation of an unsaturated market in which the principal imperative is to produce more and more. The operational structure rejects most personal potential and abilities and seeks to secure only the proper execution of delineated tasks. This was especially true at the front lines of the organization but was also largely the case in management. The four variables tended to created uniformity among skills and abilities, eliminating those that did not serve the purpose of "proper execution." They prevailed within every system, even those associated with a socialist ideology that, in principle, opposed the social and personal consequences of such a work organization.

These variables proved to be relatively consistent over a very long time, but the labor movement challenged them from the beginning, as did rapid technical and cultural evolution.

But recent changes posed the definitive challenge — namely, market saturation in industrialized countries and rapid development of the competitive economy. This new situation often demands innovation rather than large-scale production, products adapted to special requirements rather than traditional products, and ample organizational flexibility rather than a rigid operational structure.

With this profound change, uniform skills and abilities lost their appeal. In the new competitive market, knowing how to observe dysfunctions, study problems, experiment with possible solutions, and innovate on technical and organizational levels become more important than performing tasks. This is particularly true in management, where many new functions have been introduced. But the same need to diversify skills is felt on the front lines as well.

Critical as it is, this need encounters some tough obstacles. How can companies diversify skills when traditional constraints impose the criteria of specialization and proper execution of tasks? Or when the authority to use new skills and abilities is held not by the work units but by administrative departments, corporate management, and labor organizations?

Within the corporate hierarchy, obstacles are particularly persistent. In fact, uniformity of skills and abilities generally goes hand in hand with an extremely hierarchical organization of professional relationships. When there are only minor differences in the nature of skills and abilities, employees are differentiated from one another by rank and by the unequal power accorded to them by that rank.

Under highly competitive conditions, however, neither uniformity of skills and abilities nor an extremely hierarchical ordering of relationships guarantees economic success. On the contrary, the new market demands diverse, complementary skills, even on the front lines. Such skills harness personal aptitudes. An inquisitive person may develop observation skills; a jack-of-all-trades may be directed toward innovation; a foreman with a strong personality, like Raymond Dupont, may be drawn toward experimentation.

But the old rigid organization, which appears extremely conservative in the new economic context, resists the need to diversify skills. That would require abandoning the principle of specialization — as well as different pay scales and special bonuses, which are inherent in hierarchical organizations.

As a result, the requirements of the new competitive market most often clash with the conservative organization of work, the least dynamic of the four variables. This conservatism is so strong that it is still relatively rare to see companies adopt new principles of organization to make themselves better suited to survive sharp fluctuations and major changes in the business environment.

Nevertheless, successful and ongoing experiments do exist in ample numbers. They all have one point in common: they seek to base company operations on highly motivated employees. Thus, they reverse the logic of the old organization (as in Raymond Dupont's case), in which employees adapted to the work load, which was assigned according to technical and output standards.

The new principles, in contrast, integrate personal aptitudes, recognizing that in competitive conditions, they represent a valuable flexibility factor. These new principles include

- Collective output
- A combination of production steps within a job
- Individual responsibility for company success
- Overlapping functions on the operating level.

These organizational principles reflect not only new competitive market demands but also the cultural advances of recent decades. Together they can create a new balance among the four dominant variables.

Motivation as a Function of Operational Structure

What mechanisms create harmony within the organizational structure? The basis for all motivation is personal potential, which varies from one individual to another. This creative individualism is shaped by genetic predisposition, as well as by education and training. A person's potential is therefore at once a gift and an attainment.

Realizing potential does not occur automatically, except in those rare cases where gifts are much greater than attainments. In most instances, however, the socioeconomic environment demands creative individualism, which develops through use.

Potential is realized particularly in certain areas that are unique to each individual, such as a talent for music or mathematics. Creative individualism, applied in a specific area, is a personal aptitude. Sometimes referred to as ability, predisposition, or quality, it is developed through study and experience.

A person possessing a particular aptitude usually has a natural inclination to use it. This is experienced as an intense, stimulating emotional state: this is internal motivation. People who use their aptitudes feel stimulated, which leads them to make rapid progress and demonstrate their innovative and creative abilities.

But sometimes circumstances in life and work prevent people from using their aptitudes or make it difficult to do so. Or work may require them to perform tasks in areas where they have no talent or aptitude.

In these situations, personal aptitudes conflict with the restrictions of the work environment's operational structure. A bank employee with a flair for synthesis who lacks authority to handle certain cases is frustrated when he must turn them over to a department manager. The meticulous employee working on a piecework quota basis is unsatisfied because she must produce quantity, even though fine-tuning and quality are her interests.

The jack-of-all-trades assigned to an assembly line must stifle his inclination to think through and solve problems because he must do repetitive assembly work. A musically gifted student who must study law may be plagued for his entire law career by his thwarted dreams, and the enthusiastic researcher assigned management responsibilities will be deeply dissatisfied.

Whenever using one's aptitudes proves to be impossible or nearly so, the stimulating emotional state of internal motivation will be unable to be established. Stifling aptitudes ultimately brings on a different affective state — dissatisfaction or frustration — which replaces the original one.

This psychological process can be observed in all social classes and all levels of the corporate hierarchy, on the job and in private life. When a potential that was initially creative encounters obstacles that prevent it from being used and developed, it becomes negative, even destructive. The meticulous worker will ultimately grow weary of the quota system, the researcher will become frustrated or aggressive as a manager, and the jack-of-all-trades will shift his focus of interest away from his assembly-line job.

The same process holds true for society as a whole. The citizens of a district or region, threatened by crisis but unable to take initiative at the local level because decisions are made by high-level politicians far away, will ultimately adopt an attitude of criticism or revolt. This has already occurred several times since the early 1970s.

Personal motivation is therefore a function of the type of operational structure adopted by organizations and society. In practice, this relationship produces the phenomenon of behavioral metamorphosis when using personal aptitudes becomes impossible:

1. Internal motivation encounters obstacles
2. A feeling of frustration gradually develops

3. Motivation vanishes or shifts
4. Various negative attitudes are adopted.

The onset of negative attitudes means that personal aptitudes are stifled by the operational structure in the work environment and that internal motivation is replaced by feelings of dissatisfaction and frustration.

Some people attempt to escape this unpleasant feeling. Some quit their jobs, despite material advantages. Others substitute ambitions within the corporate hierarchy for their true motivation (the phenomenon of identification with the operational structure) and often become dissatisfied managers. Still others join unions so that they can express their dissatisfaction through social action. The majority simply shift their focus to non-work-related interests and become passive in their work. When compensation is lacking, however, such attitudes can also become callous, critical, or violent. This is often the source of interpersonal and company labor conflicts.

But if the organizational structure accepts and makes use of workers' aptitudes, no behavioral metamorphosis occurs. When aptitudes are utilized, potential is achieved. If the researcher can become involved in experiments, if the meticulous person and the jack-of-all-trades are given tasks and responsibilities that use these qualities, internal motivation will play a positive role.

Depending on whether personal aptitudes are accepted or rejected in the work environment, two major tendencies are observed, as shown in Figure 1. Financial outcomes, measured in terms of cost, quality, and productivity, and organizational outcomes, measured in terms of turnover, atmosphere, and conflict, will differ greatly in the two instances. In extremely competitive economic situations, this difference often determines success or failure.

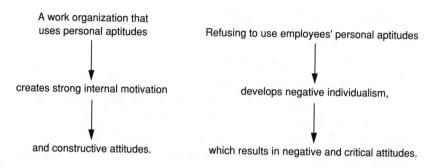

Figure 1.

Organizational Conservatism Blocks Personal Aptitudes

If the financial and organizational advantages of harnessing personal aptitudes are so significant, why refuse to do so? This phenomenon, which runs counter to common sense, is related to the nature of the organization of work, which dictates that certain aptitudes will be used and others rejected.

Each organization is designed on the basis of an underlying principle, various nuances of which play a role in its implementation. But the principle is itself determined by the characteristics and imperatives of the market — that is, by the relationship between supply and demand.

Until the early twentieth century, the relative scarcity and inadequate technological level of the means of production in Western Europe gave rise to intensive specialization of labor, which was later termed *compartmentalized work*. This approach had a definite utility at the time, for it facilitated increases in productivity. The concept of productivity continues to be associated with that principle, even in competitive conditions, although it is no longer necessarily productive and profitable.

The sequence in Figure 2 shows the profound conservatism of organizational methods. The primacy of productivity and profitability, created in a bygone era, has survived intervening

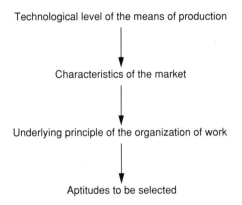

Figure 2.

societal changes. Intensive specialization of jobs and functions, which dictates rigid application of aptitudes, is still the basis for organization of work. This is true in Western Europe and North America and also in Third World countries and in countries claiming to be socialist and professing an ideology that opposes the practical effects of this principle. Moreover, the negative effects of this principle are found in all fields of endeavor — in industrial firms, business enterprises, academia, hospitals, and banks.

But other reasons explain the profound conservatism of the organizational principle that is most commonly used today. Means of production are now designed around this principle, an unnecessary approach dictated by tradition. One need only observe a machining line or assembly line to be convinced of this.

The nearly century-old tradition is so strong that even the operation of government organizations — from the national level to town halls — and of educational institutions, hospitals, and banks is based on specialization of jobs and functions.

Reducing front-line jobs to a role of simple task execution gave rise, over several decades, to a support apparatus designed to take responsibility for disturbances in the continuity of that execution. Such responsibilities include organizing the work load, allocating the work load to jobs, evaluating output, gathering and distributing information as orders and instructions, problem solving, and quality control.

These roles made it possible at the turn of the century to specialize the various phases in the completion of tasks but have subsequently become intrusive. Because of their highly structured and institutionalized nature, they now inhibit evolution in the jobs of both blue- and white-collar employees.

Now that computers make large numbers of middle-management employees unnecessary, surplus staff in that support apparatus could be directed toward more productive work. Such a reorientation is not easy, however, because the apparatus is extremely complex, especially in large companies. It has accumulated three types of responsibilities:

- Operational or horizontal responsibilities for various phases of the work process
- Hierarchical or vertical responsibilities exercised by numerous levels of management
- Corporate or organizational responsibilities for personnel management and relations with employee representatives.

This triple specialization gave rise over the decades to horizontal or functional partitioning, vertical dependency relationships, and parallel tracks with regard to wage negotiations.

Such a complex operational structure is often reinforced by a minutely detailed organization chart that determines rights and reciprocal obligations. Such charts are common in large companies in manufacturing and service industries. Finally, a system of wages, classifications, and promotion often ill-suited to the imperatives of a competitive market provides relative coherence for that set of mechanisms.

This phenomenon currently represents a genuine resistance to change. The habits of nearly a century have allowed feelings of prestige and hierarchical values to play a compensatory role, enabling workers to substitute ambition within the organizational hierarchy for unfulfilled personal motivation.

The French government's tradition of centralization clearly reinforces conservatism. Labor unions built their strategy on the harmful effects of specialization of labor and, ironically, have ultimately become attached to maintaining the compartmentalized operational structure to safeguard their role within companies and organizations.

Cries of alarm uttered since the early 1920s about the harmful effects of a compartmentalized work organization went unheeded. Theories of cultural decline were formulated to explain this extraordinary waste of human energy in the name of technological productivity.

But neither labor strife nor ideological disputes changed the essential issue. The basic principle underlying the organization of work and of society survived technological, social, and cultural change. It also survived political changes in countries that professed an ideology dedicated to overcoming social injustice.

The conservatism of social and occupational organization ultimately survived all attempts at change. It survived until the arrival of recent economic changes, which are unraveling its consistency and challenging its *raison d'être* — productivity.

What could not be achieved over several decades by social conflict, philosophical disputes, and political upheaval seems to be possible now because of the economic changes occurring.

Intense specialization and rigid application of aptitudes no longer ensure productivity and profitability under the new competitive market conditions. Indeed, sharply fluctuating work loads, short product service life, and the increasingly strong diversification of customer requirements demand not only high-performance equipment but also a flexible organization that can adapt to varying technological and business requirements. Using personal aptitudes, at the operational and other levels, can provide an organization with this essential flexibility.

CHAPTER TWO

Motivation: A Function of the Organizational System

Motivation Is Shaped by Correlations Between Market Conditions and the Company's Operational Structure

In the wake of such a rapid historical development, we shall attempt to define the principal correlations between several critical variables. The utilization of a particular aptitude in one's work is especially dependent upon these correlations.

Western European and North American markets remained unsaturated for a long time but became highly competitive in the early 1970s. Each of these large-scale market trends requires appropriate organizational principles. Intensive specialization of tasks works well in an unsaturated market, but individualization of jobs is better suited to a competitive market. The underlying principle in the first situation calls for highly selective use of abilities; in the second, responsibilities are distributed according to ability and qualifications.

If, however, we continue to apply the old organizational principle despite a change in the nature of the market, market imperatives will tend to reject that principle. Signs of this phenomenon are the dysfunctions that we often try to overcome through remedial measures.

From this interaction, these correlations arise:

- what is required (appropriate organizational principles)
- what is rejected (inappropriate principles that result in dysfunctions)
- remedial measures (attempts to overcome the inadequacy)

Figure 3 illustrates the application of these principles to saturated and unsaturated markets. As the top row shows, an unsaturated market, in which the supply does not meet the growing demand, requires application of the specialization principle (quadrant 11), which is well suited to large-scale production and the repetitive tasks of service industries. This type of market rejects the principle of individualization of jobs (quadrant 12) and is therefore a rigid, standardized organizational structure.

Organizational principles / The market	(1) Specialization	(2) Individualization	(3) Remedies
(1) Unsaturated	(11) required	(12) rejected	(13) social programs
(2) Competitive	(21) rejected	(22) required	(23) organizational programs

Figure 3. Market/Organizational Matrix

But as employees' cultural and occupational levels rise, antagonism begins to develop between personal potential and the operational structure of offices and production units. Companies often adopt enhanced social benefits as a remedy for this situation: the well-known practice of "buying" corporate harmony grants a growing number of fringe benefits. Personal and collective dissatisfaction — the main source of conflict — may evoke an enormous "corporatist" response (quadrant 13).

The second row of Figure 3 presents a different situation. When production capacity exceeds demand, the market becomes competitive and values innovation, fine-tuning of products, and adaptation of products to customers' special requirements.

Equipment must be capable of increasing the variety of product lines and models without additional cost. Organizations must be flexible, and employees must make small continuous improvements, produce high-quality products, and reduce non-value-adding costs. A competitive market increasingly rejects rigid, standardized methods of organization and intensive specialization of tasks (quadrant 21) because they are neither profitable nor productive. It requires flexibility — individualized jobs based on personal aptitudes (quadrant 22).

Without flexibility, dysfunctions occur. Attempts may be made to compensate for deficiencies by further automating equipment if there is available capital. Organizational remedies might include individual resourcefulness to circumvent pointless rules, accumulation of buffer stocks, and formation of special skill groups and production teams. This kind of remedial organizational system has development potential; its major drawback, as we shall see, is that it significantly increases unproductive costs (quadrant 23).

These relationships also apply in the context of governmental and political organizations. If the civil service continues to operate under the principle of intensive specialization of tasks and centralized decision making despite profound changes in the economic environment, antagonism could arise between the pressure of the competitive economy and the nature of governmental organization. Such antagonism appeared in the early 1970s, when local governments in France were weak and lacked power to initiate action. The central government had to set up a remedial apparatus to save companies and regions that were at risk of failure (quadrant 23).

Figure 4 highlights and summarizes the correlations between the two organizational principles and the degree to which each uses personal aptitudes. A highly specialized organizational system (quadrant 2) rigidly selects abilities and reduces their field of application to a few repetitive procedures (see row 2 of the figure). This stifles internal motivation and imposes external motivation in the form of various restrictions. Under this scenario, individualism becomes negative, and the attitudes adopted are equally negative (quadrants 21, 22, 23).

The individual Organiza- tion of work	(1) Potential (aptitudes)	(2) Motivation	(3) Attitudes adopted
(1) Individualized	(11) requires creative individualism	(12) requires internal motivation	(13) requires con- structive attitudes
(2) Specialized	(21) fosters negative individualism	(22) employs external motivation	(23) produces negative attitudes

Figure 4. Organization/Individual Matrix

Row 1 of the figure illustrates the influence of the competitive market, which increasingly requires an individualized organization and distributes tasks according to personal aptitudes. Such a practice draws on employees' creative individualism and internal motivation and results in employees adopting constructive attitudes (quadrants 11, 12, 13).

The same correlations are observed in banks, academic institutions, hospitals, and governmental and political organizations.

For example, a highly centralized and specialized governmental organization rejects local initiatives (or local potential), creating an expectation of assistance and dependence on that assistance. Such feelings destroy internal motivation. When people expect everything to come from higher up, the attitudes adopted on the local level — in municipalities or regions, in agriculture or metallurgy — will be negative or even violent.

But governmental organizations, too, can individualize. They can decentralize and transfer responsibilities to local government or professional organizations, abandon the ad hoc problem solving practiced by bureaucracies, create an information and prevention role, revise their regulations in various areas (usually done only after catastrophes or labor conflicts), and concentrate the efforts of public officials on operational problems.

The competitive market has created a situation in which different political movements are confronted directly at the local level with practical problems to be solved. A number of countries provide examples of how the different movements can coexist and even cooperate, especially when public opinion assesses political parties by their ability to stimulate and manage cooperation among different interest groups.

Strong Employees Can Change Negative Correlations

Although it is often still true that an inappropriate organizational structure stifles creative individualism (Figure 4, quadrants 21, 23) and prevents employees from helping their company more effectively, it is equally true that individual employees can successfully reverse negative trends. Such trends are not inalterable.

Even in an environment of intensive specialization of jobs and tasks, one often finds teams, and even production units and departments, in which a manager — often on the front lines — unofficially applies an innovative organizational principle.

Employees in a bank branch gradually may be given broader responsibility so that they can resolve even unusual and special issues. In assembly work normally performed according to a specialized division of tasks, operators in a production unit also may do assembly and sometimes even do complete assembly.

Most often, the corporate hierarchy is scarcely aware of this type of deviation. When the deviation ultimately represents a real solution, however, it is tolerated, even if this creates administrative complications in managing the staff. Then, if the company's market or financial situation deteriorates, the deviation can even be "discovered" as an example to be followed. This was true in the case of Raymond Dupont, the machine shop foreman described in the Introduction.

This means that within an official organizational system one often can find small islands of informal or unofficial organizational systems that are tolerated or ignored because they are more efficient than the official system. These cases are abundant in governmental organizations. Most often, they represent informal parallel channels that circumvent official channels, which are slow and detached from reality. Informal channels are often based on preferential relationships. In the context of a highly centralized bureaucracy, such remedial methods often are more efficient than official channels.

The same situation often occurs in industrial plants, business firms, and the service industry. When the official organization becomes inappropriate and produces negative trends, as indicated by dysfunctions, people try to counteract the situation in one of two ways: by taking measures that are remedial (Figure 3, quadrant 23) but do not suppress unfavorable trends or by replacing the operational structure with a different structure that is better suited to the company's requirements.

This is generally the work of employees with strong personalities. Quite often, however, such work is unofficial and informal because the work organization itself strongly resists change.

Our example is drawn from the plant of the foreman discussed previously, although similar situations can be found in manufacturing and service companies in most industries.

In the plant's purchasing office there were three work groups, each with about a dozen employees. The work was administrative and organized according to the principle of job specialization. Employees did incomplete sets of work, and the group leader had sole responsibility for choosing from several possible solutions. He also signed all documents. When large sums of money were involved, documents required the signature of the manager. It was a classic operational structure, with horizontal as well as vertical specialization (see quadrants 21, 22, and 23 in Figure 4).

Without responsibility and an overall view of the work process, employees behaved cautiously. Still, they made mistakes. Group leaders supervised them, corrected mistakes, and penalized false steps. The atmosphere was tense, and motivation was external, fed by the fear of making mistakes and being penalized.

Two groups worked under rules of the rigid organizational system. Officially, nothing distinguished the third group, the one farthest from the manager's office, from the other two groups, but it operated under an informal organization that individualized tasks.

How did this deviation from the rule come about? The third group leader realized that penalties were not an effective way to eliminate mistakes on the job because mistakes often were caused by a narrow view of procedures and limited responsibility in each job. He tactfully transformed group meetings into training sessions at which employees showed coworkers which procedures they followed and also discussed hypothetical work situations that might arise. Through this apprenticeship employees gained occupational know-how.

In the second phase of the session, each employee selected tasks according to his or her knowledge and abilities. Those who had an inclination for long, complex procedures could have them, and those who liked shrewd negotiations chose tasks that allowed them to deal with suppliers.

In this way, motivation was freed from the customary external restrictions of compartmentalized, specialized tasks. In short, the group leader informally replaced his company's principle of work organization with another principle better suited to market conditions and the internal motivations of group members. Management hardly noticed the change, but it did recognize the group's results, which surpassed those of other groups.

These experiments are usually very limited spatially. Nevertheless, they are of significant interest because they anticipate an evolution of the company's operational structure by informally devising a work organization that is well suited to the complexities of a competitive market. In most instances, both approaches are found within the same company, as shown in Figure 4:

- quadrants 21, 22, and 23 exemplify the official organizational scheme (used by most departments and production units)
- quadrants 11, 12, and 13 foreshadow a new organizational scheme that is more productive and more motivating than the first.

Generally speaking, however, the official organizational scheme's conservatism and resistance to change isolate these promising trends, so that they remain in enclaves.

Socioeconomic Influences on Motivation

During periods of great socioeconomic change, conflicting, even antagonistic, trends generally surface. The tendency for work relationships and the organization of work to lag significantly in relation to other determining variables has proven troublesome for many Western firms since the early 1970s.

When the inability to adapt to a new, complex situation presents a major obstacle, a remedial organizational scheme develops (Figure 3, quadrant 23). Instead of providing a solution, however, it postpones the problem of inevitable change. In addition, by increasing both the labor surplus and the burden of unproductive costs, such schemes run the risk of further intensifying the problems.

The small islands and enclaves that experiment with effective and lasting solutions (Figure 4, quadrants 11, 12, 13) are early indicators of a new correlation among the variables, heralding the end of the dysfunctions. These large-scale trends are the subject of the following chapters, where they are described in detail through the example of Raymond Dupont.

The rigid official operational structure of the large factory where Dupont worked was based on a generalized application of the principle of specialization of jobs and functions. As far back as the late 1960s, this demotivating organizational scheme was becoming increasingly unsuited to the new technical and commercial constraints (see Figure 3, quadrants 21, 22).

Instead of conducting an in-depth diagnosis, however, plant managers called for remedial measures to resolve the growing number of dysfunctions (Figure 3, quadrants 13, 23).

At the same time, a flexible operational structure based on employee motivation was attempted in a few localized experiments. Raymond Dupont's experiment succeeded in completely reversing the old trend. In this team, where previously *machines* were the priority and employees worked under an individual piecework output system, negative individualism had become highly developed (Figure 4, quadrants 21, 22, 23). The situation changed radically, as the foreman successfully — and illicitly — instituted a collective output system within his team and implemented an individualized organizational scheme (Figure 4, quadrants 11, 12, 13).

This type of adaptation happens in various industrial sectors, in companies in the service industries, and in government organizations, regardless of local conditions. Collective responsibility can be created in a department or working group. In an industrial unit, the members of a department can become involved in the distribution of tasks, and a collective output system can replace an individual output system.

Despite the differences in environment, the motivating effects of the change in operational structure will be comparable. The machine shop foreman's action is therefore typical of its kind.

This successful experiment ultimately emerged from its underground status as a result of a sudden worsening in the plant's financial problems. It was the beginning of a profound change that quickly transformed the machining area and strongly motivated workers in the production units.

CHAPTER THREE

Stages in the Creation of Motivation

The parallel between the story of the plant and the large-scale trends that occur in periods of socioeconomic change is developed and described in later chapters. Before beginning that presentation, however, we elaborate on the factors shaping motivation. In the work environment, this process is usually guided by three centers of influence.

The Three Motivational Centers of Influence

The successive psychological stages in developing creative individualism — the substance of motivation — are heavily influenced by a person's professional environment. This relationship develops from constant interaction with others.

An internally motivated individual desires to use his or her abilities and may be either assisted in or thwarted from doing so by the operational structure of the work environment. If assisted, the relationship between the individual and the work environment is harmonious; if thwarted, however, a conflict situation arises.

A job — which represents a person's most direct contact with the company — exerts the primary influence in developing motivation. When an employee's job description corresponds to his or her abilities, that person will be internally motivated to practice creative individualism. But without a correspondence, creative individualism becomes negative.

Inclusion or exclusion of various powers and authority within job descriptions determines whether employees identify with their company's goals. If the distribution of power and authority draws on basic personal abilities, employees will align themselves with company goals. Such allegiance is reinforced by receiving technical, business, and financial information that involves employees in the company's business results.

Generally speaking, employees are influenced by three centers within the organizational structure:

- The job and its task
- The authority, duties, and responsibilities of the job
- Information on the company's business results.

Motivation is clearly an individual psychological process, but that process closely interacts with the work environment and its centers of influence:

- Individualizing a job allows personal abilities to be applied broadly and stimulates the development of creative individualism.
- Transferring authority, duties, and responsibilities to the person who carries out the job further motivates and broadens an employee's field of activity.
- Finally, associating jobs with knowledge of the company's financial and business situation reinforces the ongoing process of motivation.

These three centers of influence are overlapping and complementary. Jobs in and of themselves, even when individualized, cannot create a well-developed sense of responsibility and financial judgment. Likewise, widely distributed informational bulletins and company newsletters have no lasting effect if individualized jobs and decision-making authority do not provide a solid foundation (see Figure 5).

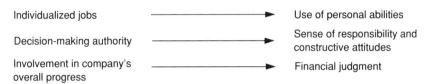

Individualized jobs	Use of personal abilities
Decision-making authority	Sense of responsibility and constructive attitudes
Involvement in company's overall progress	Financial judgment

Figure 5.

Today's economic conditions call for management to take action to eliminate the obstacles that hinder the expression and expansion of creative individualism and to encourage and support the experiments conducted by strong managers. Companies that adapt to these new conditions enhance their ability to compete.

Jobs: The Starting Point

A job, particularly on the front lines of the organization, is the point of connection for all work-related activity. It is a set of operations as well as an emotional tie to the company.

Employees are deeply influenced by their jobs. The content of a job may be rich and varied or composed of short, fragmented production steps. It can isolate an employee or put him or her in contact with people in other jobs, other departments, or higher levels of authority.

A job may be viewed as neutral, objective, or impersonal when the principle of specialization is applied, as was the case during the long period of rapid growth. But it also can be viewed as a forum for implementing the employee's abilities and aptitudes.

The behavioral reactions of employees differ considerably depending on which approach is chosen. With an approach that is based on specialization, job analysis, classification, and qualification are important functions, especially in large firms in the manufacturing and service industries. Such tasks are handled by many departments, which are usually part of the personnel management structure. Even today, grids and various techniques are used to systematize jobs and divide them into different tasks according to technical or theoretical requirements, complexity, and importance.

The long period of rapid growth created economic stability, and the slow technological progress of that period meant a long life for products and services. In the absence of well-developed competition, customer requirements were not as varied as they are now. At that time, job descriptions could be neutral or impersonal and not account for the personalities of individual employees.

In the context of a competitive market, however, where small improvements made at the working level often give rise to new products and generate savings on unproductive costs, job descriptions need to be based on the principle of creative individualism.

In this complete reversal of the customary approach, departments traditionally in charge of personnel management transfer much of their power and authority to the lowest level of management and retain only the roles related to advice, information, and planning.

Indeed, if it is well prepared for such a task, the lowest level of management is the best place for creating harmony between job requirements and personal abilities. Under competitive conditions, however, those on the front lines and their supervisors need not only individualized jobs but also other powers and responsibilities that remain scattered horizontally (according to operational structure or function) and vertically (according to corporate hierarchy).

Such a transfer of authority has now become possible — and indeed necessary — because of the rapid technological development of the communications media and production methods. Computerized information need no longer trickle down through official channels to production units and offices. Instead, it can be routed directly to wherever it is needed for practical purposes.

To attract and keep customers, insurance companies and banks need to handle specific cases without delay. In industrial firms, changes in production schedules and special customer requirements create many "disturbances" that cannot be settled in the upper levels of management. Action must be taken where the practical problems arise.

In both instances, the responsibilities that are often dispersed among administrative offices and upper management must be regrouped at the lowest level of management and in working groups at the operational level of the organization. This is an economic necessity; it is above all a matter of motivation. Individualizing jobs and regrouping powers and responsibilities are effective methods of reinforcing creative individualism, which is the basis for substantial employee involvement.

The process involves profound change, and change usually produces resistance from those who must move on to more productive work, as well as from those who must leave the narrow confines of specialized jobs but regard such a maneuver with suspicion.

This dual resistance often delays the inevitable change — that is, redistributing duties, responsibilities, and authority and redirecting employees toward work that is important under competitive market conditions.

Typical Strategies for Action

What approaches to achieving change are usually adopted by companies in the manufacturing and service industries? The choice generally is determined by the nature and intensity of the resistance to change and the balance of power in labor relations, but the following strategies are most generally used:

- Negotiation (particularly when there is strong labor representation)
- Top-down action (when management uses a central plan)
- Bottom-up action (when a middle manager with a strong personality achieves a profound change at the local level, generally without the support of the upper management).

In smaller companies, the last two approaches complement each other and quite often are intermingled. In these situations, adaptation to competitive market requirements and unleashing individual creativity can occur rapidly.

In larger companies in which the proliferation of administrative, management, and organizational powers created a sprawling organization, the process of shifting authority is generally slow and rife with conflict. The strategy of negotiation rarely succeeds, since labor representation has not yet undergone its own change. Top-down action runs the risk of causing blockages, particularly when authority, duties, and responsibilities are to be withdrawn or transferred elsewhere. And bottom-up action is rarely used in large firms because management, removed from the front lines by a multitude of hierarchical levels, usually ignores successful experiments.

Figure 6 summarizes three typical strategies for motivating employees to increase their input and highlights the advantages and disadvantages of each in the context of both rigid and individualized organizational systems.

Management of smaller companies is interested in "discovering" experiments that were successful at the bottom levels, because such bottom-up action anticipates change, charts the course to be followed, and by its very example decreases resistance to change.

Strategy Organiza- tional system	Negotiation	Top-down action	Bottom-up action
Rigid, specialized	Difficult and costly	Produces resistance to change	Practiced by managers with strong personalities
Individualized	Facilitated by staff participation	Represents a developmental plan	Occurs on an ongoing basis and sets up phases for gradual and continuous development

Figure 6.

This type of action is especially significant at the first stage in the creation of motivation — individualizing jobs. It is often equally pronounced, however, at the second stage — transferring (or regaining) certain practical duties, responsibilities, and authority to the front lines.

In Raymond Dupont's successful experiment, the workers on his team — without the support of corporate management — entered the areas reserved for certain administrative departments and the upper levels of management. They occupied the territory, as it were, by eliminating the need for intervention by those who previously assumed responsibility for the team's special problems. Only later, after the "discovery" of this outcome, were particular administrative, management, and organizational powers formally transferred to the first level of management and the team.

Such experiments in bottom-up action are more numerous than one may think. Strong internal motivation does exist at the first level of middle management in industrial facilities as well as the service industry. Still, management first must notice it; only then can it be analyzed and integrated into management's development strategy.

The Old Concept: Organized Stifling of Motivation

Using internal motivation liberates employees from job constraints. This is relatively easy to accomplish in small companies but proves difficult in large corporations. After nearly a century, increasingly varied constraints have accumulated to create a virtual barrier around jobs that nips employees' creativity in the bud.

Some of these constraints are inherent in the principle of specialization. Rigid organizations standardize jobs and compartmentalize not only manual tasks but also tasks that are mental, administrative, or organizational. They also fragment responsibilities and specialize functions.

Other constraints are the product of a half-century of corporate regulation — a result of the collaboration of lawmakers and unions — that sets forth employees' rights and obligations in minute detail.

Whether the origin of such constraints is technological or legislative, or whether their intention is to specialize tasks and functions or set limits on employees' responsibilities, they nonetheless reduce the areas in which individuals can exercise their personal abilities.

Private ownership of the means of production in the capitalist economic system is sometimes pointed to as the origin of these constraints, but this approach ignores other determining factors, such as the formerly low technological level of the means of production or the characteristics of an unsaturated market. Yet the same organizational constraints burden jobs in systems where the means of production are entirely nationalized.

Constraints on internal motivation fall into four general categories:

- The scope and context of the job: This includes schedule, work hours, work load, hierarchical organization of tasks, output, and required quality.

- The range of job responsibilities: Anything that interferes with regular, steady performance — such as unforeseen procedures, unusual problems, preparation, procurement of supplies, or deciding among multiple solutions — is eliminated. Such tasks are viewed as separate responsibilities and are turned into administrative or management functions, which inevitably place the job in a vast net of dependent relationships.
- The qualifications, professional category, status, and seniority of the job: These constraints function not only as restrictions but as "rights" that confer a value on the content of the job. More often than not, this determines the compensation associated with the job.
- The rapport between worker and job: Is the person adapting to restrictions? Is his or her attitude disciplined or passive? Does he or she make mistakes? These constraints are examples of organizational and management functions, such as issuing penalties, recommending promotions, performing evaluations, and exercising control over discipline and output, and so on.

A Difficult Matching Between Abilities and Job Requirements

How do people view the strict delimitation and regulation of their jobs when these constraints prevent them from using their innate abilities? When there is disharmony — when the constraints become insurmountable obstacles and the employee feels cornered and locked into an inextricable tangle of constraints — protective attitudes appear. One such attitude is avoidance. The employee tries to have his or her job changed. In extreme cases, the person quits.

Another attitude, which appears particularly after unsuccessful attempts to flee, is resignation. The employee settles into the constraints and copes with them. He or she tries to ensure ample maneuvering space despite the job's restrictions by perfecting the work methods or by making small improvements that streamline the job. That way, the employee has good output but also has additional time to rest. These innovations and streamlinings, which are often interesting and clever, are usually hidden; quite often, the employee's coworkers and immediate supervisor do not notice them.

Those who cannot escape from their job or do not manage it with small improvements often adopt an aggressive attitude. They appear to be disagreeable, dissatisfied grumblers who are eventually left alone to work at their own pace. They may not be disagreeable people but may use an aggressive attitude as a weapon for lack of other means. When such an attitude becomes pointless, as it did in Raymond Dupont's team, they simply abandon it, demonstrating that it is game-playing rather than a character trait.

The last attitude toward constraint commonly adopted is to search for fulfillment elsewhere. Employees may become absorbed in non-job-related interests, ambition to climb the corporate ladder, or union activity. Without this kind of sublimation or protective attitude, negative individualism usually arises.

Compatibility between job requirements (or constraints) and personal abilities is significant, but it rarely results from a match between a job description and individual abilities. More often, the employee has secretly modified the job by widening his or her field of activity, increasing his or her value or importance, or altering relationships with those who hold authority.

For example, an administrative clerk whose job is to store and arrange microfiche in a technical office soon realizes that his status and qualifications are low in relation to the technical personnel. His feeling of inferiority pushes him to increase the value of his job by implementing a rational but very complex system of organization. When impatient technicians cannot find information, they must call on his services, and he soon becomes indispensable to them. By entering the domain of other professional categories (technicians, in this case), he breaks through the barrier erected by his original job description, expands his responsibilities, and gains higher status.

Such situations of job alteration to match the employee's ambitions occur most often at the management level. Even in the lower levels of the organization, however, similar attempts are often made to get around the constraints of the job.

More significant are the examples in which a lower-level manager, such as Raymond Dupont, the machine shop foreman, without express authority adapts jobs and their constraints to new technical or economic data. These cases often involve major innovations that experiment with organizational methods well suited to the requirements of the competitive market.

Managers confronted with difficult situations may be led to innovate. By rising above the narrow confines of their function and embarking on experiments, they appropriate authority and responsibility to eliminate constraints that hinder work efficiency and stifle their subordinates' creativity.

Such bottom-up actions presuppose the approval of members of a department or team. This is not easy to achieve because accepting job constraints is a deeply ingrained pattern and hierarchical acquired rights ultimately influence employee behavior. But if group approval is won, deep-seated reforms can be implemented, and jobs can become flexible and adaptable to personal abilities. Middle managers in departments and teams then can implement various organizational systems that create harmony between workers and their jobs, including the following:

- Collective responsibility for departmental work load
- Collective output
- Distribution of tasks according to personal abilities
- Collective evaluation of unusual problems
- Collective appraisal of departmental functioning.

These reforms are based on the internal motivation that individuals have to use their abilities. In fact, in most jobs some requirements are not "covered": they have aspects that the employee satisfies little or not at all, and employees have abilities that their jobs do not require. Quite often the employee-job relationship is not completely harmonious and can result in antagonism. The more numerous these uncovered job requirements and dormant personal abilities, the more frustration experienced by workers.

But if tasks are chosen according to abilities, and a legal — or even illicit — reform makes it possible for employees to regain administrative and management authority and responsibility, then the employee's creative individualism can expand (see Figure 7).

In a rigid organization, certain types of management and highly organized relationships risk increasing feelings of frustration and dissatisfaction because employees are penalized for "shortcomings" in the areas represented by *a* and *b*, while their claims of ability in areas 1, 2, 3, and 4 are misinterpreted.

The risk disappears when a group leader makes an effort to individualize jobs. Front-line managers are often differentiated from managers at upper levels by their ability to grasp the personal abilities of the employees in the working ranks of the organization. The practical problems they confront, especially in a competitive situation, often develop this valuable ability to a considerable degree.

Indeed, front-line supervisors quickly realize that their department or team is composed of workers with diverse but generally complementary qualities. Such variety is a handicap in a rigid organization in which the jobs have a standard, objective, and interchangeable nature. In fact, in such cases, personal abilities do not lead to increasing administrative and management authority, duties, and responsibilities but often remain

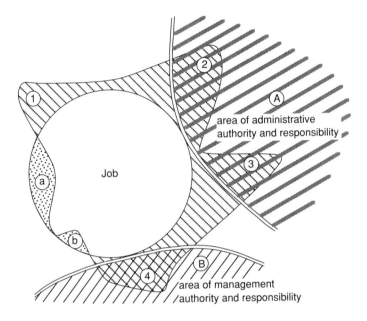

a, b = Job requirements not fulfilled by the individual

1, 2, 3, 4 = Individual abilities not used on the job

A = Area of hierarchical management authority and responsibility, where an employee
could assume responsibility (2, 3)

B = Area of administrative authority and responsibility, where an employee could also
have responsibility (4)

Figure 7.

unused, causing feelings of dissatisfaction and in time creating
negative individualism.

Transforming jobs into centers of influence for motivation
and removing constraints are challenging but essential tasks.
Under difficult economic circumstances, such changes are often
the only way to increase the competitiveness of a company
without additional investment.

PART TWO

Removing Demotivating Constraints

Under highly competitive market conditions, employee motivation is often the greatest determinant of a company's success.

Using creative individualism to bridge the gap between employee expectations and company goals makes it possible to avoid costly investments by using existing equipment more efficiently. Moreover, the work load can be adjusted to the volume of orders, and small individual improvements can generate new products.

Many companies in the manufacturing and service sectors owe their current expansion to their employees' creativity. These companies, often modest in size or newly established, hire and nurture young employees who generate fresh ideas. Their hierarchies generally are reduced to an absolute minimum, jobs are free of traditional constraints, and authority is highly decentralized. Ideas and suggestions flow freely. Management shares its plans and concerns with employees, and issues are then studied in concrete form at the operational level of the organization, where practical solutions can be tested.

An important aspect of this new type of management is to establish a continual dialogue with employees to eliminate barriers that hinder their efforts. Under today's difficult economic circumstances, this new role is becoming increasingly recognized and appreciated in public opinion.

In France, home users of the Minitel computer network can instantly register their reactions and opinions about various companies' business agreements to facilitate the adjustment of working time to market fluctuations.

Such corporate openness, facilitated by audiovisual media, is changing the image and the place of companies in modern society. It also eliminates traditional secrecy and modifies the role of labor representation, which has not yet fully adapted to the competitive market conditions facing modern companies.

Such positive evolution is already occurring rapidly in progressive companies, but in other companies, the evolution is slow. Too often, intensive specialization of jobs and functions (the essential traits of rigid organization) and the consequences of such specialization (negative individualism and labor conflict) stand in the way of progress.

In rigidly organized companies, which still represent the majority, job individualization, distribution of tasks according to personal aptitudes, and transfer of practical authority and responsibility to the front lines of the organization are blocked or occur only in spurts under the pressure of the competitive market.

Under such conditions, employees cannot initiate action. They cannot increase their input or the number of small improvements, however necessary these actions might be. Their jobs are blocked by a multitude of outmoded constraints.

In these companies, the example of strong middle managers and supervisors can trigger a positive evolution. Top management must be aware of its role in discovering these "strong points" and must integrate them into its strategic plans.

The elimination of impediments to innovation is the first stage in motivating employees, and it varies according to the different market segments of the manufacturing and service industries.

Raymond Dupont, the machine shop foreman, identified the characteristic factors of his industry and analyzed and understood their source. He succeeded in solving a costly, thorny problem of a general nature that had endured for many years. His action in an unfavorable environment (Figure 4, quadrants 21, 22) created harmony between the competitive market and the organization of his team (Figure 3, quadrant 22, and Figure

4, quadrant 11). His was a local solution to a serious problem relating to global economic change.

Dupont's results were ultimately discovered by management, which allowed the gradual transfer of practical authority and responsibility to the front lines of the organization. It also further reinforced employees' desire to exercise creative individualism in the interest of their company.

CHAPTER FOUR

Constraints that Block
Positive Job Evolution

The Difficult Process of Job Liberation

To illustrate the theoretical analysis presented in Part One, this chapter describes in detail the bottom-up action carried out by Raymond Dupont in his machine shop. This experiment has value for most market segments because it can be conducted in both manufacturing and service sector companies. The purpose of the foreman's action from the start was to free his employees' jobs from the traditional constraints that stifle creative individualism in any field of endeavor.

In the past, intensive specialization of jobs led to mixed results. Quantitative growth increased, but negative individualism and labor conflict were created as well. Under the present competitive market conditions, which require great operational flexibility and a labor-intensive approach, rigid organization has become an obstacle to growth. Such an organizational scheme stands in the way of evolution and creates resistance to change.

Within departments or teams, this evolution often occurs through individualizing jobs and regrouping certain administrative and management functions at the front-line levels.

Individualized jobs unleash creative individualism, while re-grouping functions enhances personal motivation and frees those who previously held the authority to work more effectively.

Individualizing and regrouping allow a company to become flexible and responsive to the deviations and disturbances created by the competitive market.

The failure of a rigid organization to adapt to competitive market imperatives has serious consequences, such as labor surpluses of more than 10 percent and the stifling of innovative capacity at the operating levels of the organization. These negative impacts materialize — as in the case of the foreman's plant — in the form of deteriorating prices and excess costs that may approach 20 percent.

This failure to adapt leads to indebtedness and operating deficits. The foreman's plant illustrates the typical situation, which currently exists in all segments of the market.

In addition, what seemed in the past to be simply a corporate and human imperative has become a technological and economic imperative under the new economic conditions. New communications media have made it possible to shorten operational channels as well as organizational channels, resulting in quicker, more efficient functioning and making it possible for unconstrained employees to make major improvements.

Such a transformation radically regroups the corporate hierarchy into a simpler, more transparent structure. The front-line level of management, once considered the least valuable, now gains greater importance; in fact, after the dispersed hierarchical authority and functional responsibilities have been redistributed, the front-line level embodies the entire management function.

An Experiment: Anticipating Positive Evolution
(see Figure 4, quadrants 11, 12)

The new economic perspective, which is inevitable in most market segments, provides the backdrop for Raymond Dupont's bottom-up action. With a few specific adaptations at the local level, the approach can be applied in manufacturing as well as service industry companies.

This representative experiment, which illustrates the prominent features of actions now being taken in many companies, also shows that what is valid within a team or microcosm also has a certain validity on the general level. In fact, jobs are not the only realm in which long-standing constraints have had a blocking effect. For example, small-scale savers stayed away from industrial investment for a long time, at least partly because regulations and the financial and taxation system dissuaded them from investing.

Companies enveloped by administrative and organizational constraints react slowly under competitive conditions. Contracts and orders are lost because of the slow pace dictated by procedures that are often decades old. Jobs disappear because regulations created during the long high-growth period frustrate attempts to take preventive measures.

Repealing outdated regulations and housecleaning obsolete procedures must be carried out at all levels. Encouraging and supporting such actions, particularly bottom-up actions, is a major task of management at the present time. Neither negotiation (which is too slow and hardly experimental) nor top-down action (which creates resistance to change) is sufficient in itself to accomplish such a large-scale task.

In many instances, bottom-up action is the only practical alternative. Its advantages are ease of testing hypothetical solutions and ability to reduce resistance to change. When managers discover these actions, help to implement them, and perfect them through development plans, they can significantly accelerate change and often achieve spectacular results.

The foreman's team, when freed from the usual constraints, reduced costs by more than 15 percent and almost completely recovered the losses caused earlier by the inadequate operational structure. In addition, through its growing creative individualism, the team made technological improvements and streamlined its work procedures. As the description of the experiment proceeds, we will formulate some generalizations that allow us to conceptualize the salient features of the foreman's approach.

Every manufacturing or service sector company has characteristics that are peculiar to its market segment, its products or services, its size, its personnel, and even its tradition, so the experiment described below cannot be regarded as a recipe. It does provide the following methodological know-how, however, which applies to other companies:

- Formulating the action
- Starting from the employees' expectations to avoid resistance to change
- Unblocking jobs through a collective output system
- Distributing tasks according to personal abilities
- Developing organizational procedures that foster a sense of responsibility
- Using small improvements to gain the time needed for collective analysis, and
- Regaining administrative responsibilities and management powers, which facilitates management's top-down change initiatives.

These methodological points are valid in most market segments and are developed further following the description of the foreman's experiment.

To help readers refer to the two figures in Chapter 2 that summarize the working hypotheses of this book, the figure and correlation numbers are indicated after headings in the remainder of this chapter. Readers can refer to the figures to compare the theory with Raymond Dupont's successful experiment. This connection is also reinforced by the introductions to each part of this book, which, similarly, form a continuing text that can be consulted separately.

The Team Situation Before the Experiment
(see Figure 3, quadrants 12, 13)

Raymond Dupont realized as time passed that various constraints weighed heavily on the jobs in his group and stifled internal motivation. Failure to draw on the personal abilities of workers meant not just a loss of efficiency but also signaled the advent of new problems.

In his team, that dual loss was linked directly to the old piecework system, which was based on individual output. It was a restrictive system that dictated qualifications, wages, job descriptions and duties, and promotions.

This system of work created *negative* individualism:

- Some workers argued over who would machine the easy pieces, a task that ensured good output.
- Others, who observed procedures with some difficulty, opposed timekeeping; this had become a point of contention and gave rise to labor demands.
- Job descriptions were also a source of division in the team, as were job assignments.
- Workers refused to perform duties that were not stipulated in the job descriptions; this refusal led to negotiations and even bitter conflicts.
- When the experienced workers had easy pieces to machine, they sped up their work to give themselves a few additional minutes of rest, which irritated other members of the team.
- Finally, the qualification scale gave rise to acrobatic maneuvers to enable some workers to move to higher job categories, which other members of the team viewed as favoritism.

Temporary settlements of this animosity, contention, and internal division continually engaged and mobilized the labor organizations, costing the company dearly. The foreman assessed the resultant loss at 20 percent of the manufacturing costs.

Inadequate working conditions created negative individualism, which, in turn, multiplied the already costly problems. In a perpetually tense atmosphere, employees, caught up in having their own buttons pushed, used their energy and intelligence not to help their company but to circumvent the constraints of the organization of work. They did everything possible to

- Bend the rules of personnel management
- Nibble away at the factors that separated job categories
- Ensure small advantages of all kinds
- Find relationships that made it possible to obtain better jobs.

The bad atmosphere and the negative individualism of coworkers gradually led some workers to transfer their interest to non-work-related pursuits where they could develop their individuality. Stamp collecting, gardening, sports, and other endeavors absorbed their energy and attention more effectively than their work. This was not just a "don't-give-a-damn" attitude, as management thought. Rather, it was a search for protection against the debilitating atmosphere and the internal division of the team.

Under these circumstances, the company was using only a fraction — perhaps half and in some instances a third — of the real capacity of the team. The remaining intelligence, energy, and capability were invested in negative individualism, which, far from being neutral, considerably complicated the foreman's task.

Dupont also suffered from the negative attitude of the team. But could he transform its negative individualism? Memoranda, warnings, and other actions taken by management had no effect.

His counterparts, confronted by the same problems, tried to contain the effects of negative individualism by imposing discipline. Others battled with their own managers and labor representatives. Finally, those who were already weary of the unpleasant and demotivating atmosphere abandoned the struggle and adopted a passive stance or took refuge in their own non-work-related hobbies and interests. Caught by the same psychological reflexes as their workers, the foremen went through several phases of adaptation and finally adopted some variation of negative individualism. The plant consequently lost much of its working capacity, as workers kept their output to a strict minimum.

Dupont, who had already tried all of those remedies, continued searching. His strong points included curiosity and a talent for studying different phenomena. Without management support, he threw himself into transforming the negativity of his workers' individualism into creativity. Because his actions were not sanctioned by the labor organizations or prompted by favorable conditions, they had to remain isolated and quasi-illegal. But time worked in his favor. Ongoing technological change and the competitive market, which complicated the work considerably, brought about certain changes in the plant.

This trend was not hard to notice. In fact, the foreman noticed that, for several years, his plant's product had been undergoing more and more customized modifications in response to customer demand. He also noticed that the plant's managers no longer regarded customers as anonymous consumers, as they had in the past. Instead, the customers were seen as individuals whose preferences and needs were to be seriously studied.

This trend toward customizing the product obviously complicated work on the front lines of the organization. How could a foreman meet the growing demands for shortened deadlines and improved quality with workers who invested their energy and talent in negative individualism?

Dupont also observed that such negative individualism was hardly a question of genetic predisposition. Rather, it was an acquired trait. In fact, the different kinds of demotivation (or negative individualism) in the company were determined by team organization and personnel management policies and procedures.

Front-line supervisors, however, lacked authority to manipulate these determining factors. Personnel management policies and procedures were shaped by labor organizations, and the organization of work in the machine shop depended in particular on the technical departments. The foreman occupied the lowest level in the company's hierarchical structure. His job was, essentially, to execute the production schedule and not to adapt the team structure and the personnel procedures to the new constraints of the work or to the personal qualities of his workers.

Nevertheless, to transform the negative aspects of his team members' individualism, he had to serve in that function and to do so without authorization. The risk was comparable to that of penetrating a new, unknown market or modifying a product after a market survey.

He began his course of action cautiously. As his counterparts invested their intelligence in seeking circuitous courses of action, exceptions to the rules, and remedial solutions, he acted to modify the negative attitude of his workers and transform it into creative individualism.

Knowing that the workers themselves ultimately suffered from this situation and that preoccupation with outside pursuits and internal disagreements masked deep dissatisfaction, he was able to win their trust. He undertook a course of action with them that, over several months, made it possible to replace the individual piecework system with the much more flexible collective output system.

According to the long-standing practices of the plant, however, his action was not regarded as an experiment in developing a motivating organizational scheme well suited to the difficult economic context. Instead, it was considered an infraction: the function of front-line management was principally to execute, not to experiment.

To be sure, the customer was already regarded as an individual and the product was undergoing customized modifications. But management still failed to recognize the individual qualities of the foreman or the synthesizing function that he served quite effectively.

In Dupont's system, the operational structure of the team was flexible. The organization of work adapted itself to technical problems by using personal abilities. But the old rigid organization still surrounded the team and burdened it additionally with costly end-runs around the rules and with the remedial role of upper management, which assumed responsibility for controlling the various risks occasioned by customized modifications to the product.

The foreman took risks in the interest of his team and his plant. He made innovations by sidestepping the organizational routine to test an operational structure that unleashed personal energy and unshackled jobs from their demotivating constraints, enabling each person to use his or her abilities in the work.

Two systems of organization thus existed side by side. The more efficient system used by the team, which anticipated the future, was surrounded by barriers. Everything still stood in the way of expanding that system: customs, labor-management interests, the "susceptibility" to corporate hierarchy, the remedial role of the upper levels of management, and unbending attitudes in the labor organizations.

Dupont's experiment was discovered only after the plant's business suffered a major decline. Once the experiment was acknowledged as a success, it enabled production units to abandon a remedial mode and adopt an individualized organization that motivated employees and eliminated high costs.

CHAPTER FIVE

An Experiment in Removing Blockages and Creating Motivation

Implementing an Informal but Motivating Organization

Precisely what did Raymond Dupont do? Before describing his approach in detail, we might say that Dupont developed his workers' professionalism and inquisitiveness. He used his daily contacts with them to achieve this. Workers began to substitute for each other voluntarily. When everyone knew several jobs, job rotation became possible, marking the end of work based on individual output.

All of these events occurred away from the scrutiny of management because Dupont's production unit was relatively distant from corporate offices. Since his output was rather good, he had few visitors.

Certainly, if the company's management had been able to adapt new job criteria for operators as a result of the business decline, and if innovators had been encouraged to look closely at the current structure, Dupont would have reacted otherwise. He would not have needed to take underground action protected only by his workers' complicity.

In his company, however, no such goals existed. No one yet acknowledged that motivation is shaped by or depends, above all, on the nature of the operation of the departments and teams. No one believed that, by adapting the organization of work to personal aptitudes, it is possible to achieve increased input involvement, improve production and quality, and reduce unproductive costs.

Nevertheless, an odd situation had occurred in which costs continued to rise while financial resources dwindled. Decision makers grew very nervous. How could they halt the decline in profits? How could they offset the growing costs of employee benefits? How could they increase productivity to not only offset those benefit costs but also make the company grow?

The plant could have relied on individual innovators to restructure inadequate commercial, technological, economic, and labor procedures. But in the absence of such a policy, only the old corporate hierarchical method was used, which consisted of pressure and penalties. The goal was to motivate by applying constraints.

Consequently, there were no organizational reforms in corporate management and operational departments. Omissions, errors, delays, and inadequate technical solutions inevitably drifted down to the production units with no preventive correction. Figure 8 illustrates how this situation made life difficult for the work teams.

The flexibility that the foreman brought to his team's organization of work allowed it to offset the omissions, errors, and delays that originated in the various departments. As Figure 8 shows, his team was able to respond directly to the numerous demands of customers.

A New Organization Based on Employee Expectations
(see Figure 4, quadrant 12)

Raymond Dupont succeeded in obtaining significant financial results, even under unfavorable conditions, by removing the

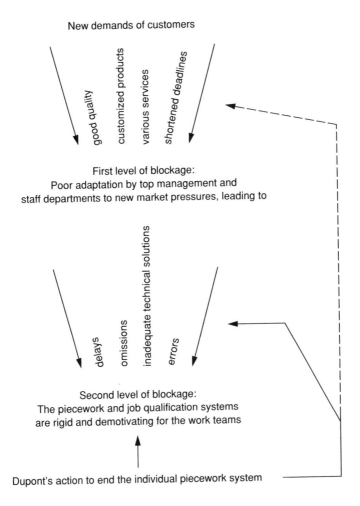

New demands of customers

good quality
customized products
various services
shortened deadlines

First level of blockage:
Poor adaptation by top management and
staff departments to new market pressures, leading to

inadequate technical solutions

delays
omissions
errors

Second level of blockage:
The piecework and job qualification systems
are rigid and demotivating for the work teams

Dupont's action to end the individual piecework system

Figure 8.

second level of blockage. Through that reform, jobs were freed
of their constraints, and creative individualism developed
rapidly within the team. He would not have been able to
achieve such results, however, without the support of his workers. The entire process was based on their relationship.

Dupont knew and respected his workers. He treated them not as subordinates in the organizational framework, but rather as people who wanted to contribute to achieving an important goal. This was the root of his "infraction."

Dupont's primary objective was to avoid the censure and criticism of his superiors, and he began by resolving the thorny problems of the output-based system of work.

This means that Dupont devoted himself *indirectly* to achieving financial goals that were not possible under the conditions established. He tackled the conditions first by diagnosing his team within the context of the two levels of blockage to uncover hidden "openings."

To undertake such a course of action, he needed the support and consent of his workers. He had to rely on their internal motivation.

Labor representatives also aspired to gain the workers' trust. To win that trust, they used every means available. They gave information to workers, for Dupont had no information to share. They came to his superiors' offices in successive waves instead of going directly to him. The labor representatives explained that the piecework output system was part of the nature of capitalism and that the management did not want to abandon it because it boosted profits.

How could an uninformed manager, literally ignored by his superiors, counter these arguments? After all, didn't they at least "explain" the existence of this long-disputed system? Ironically, this explanation was actually reinforced by orders given and pressure generated by the corporate hierarchy.

Eventually, Dupont discovered that he could act in spite of the strong competition from the labor representatives. He focused on areas where his workers showed sensitivity: the collective environment of the team, the relative monotony of the work, and demotivation. The foreman understood — and his own experience as a blue-collar worker facilitated this discovery

— that no one can spend eight hours at work when he feels ill at ease in his production unit. He also understood that wage increases did not compensate for poor job conditions: no one felt more motivated or tolerated the conditions better after an increase than they had before.

He began his course of action cautiously. Since he had no formal training, he worked primarily from experience and intuition. One day he witnessed a conversation between two workers who apparently wanted to switch jobs periodically. He seized the opportunity by covering for the two workers. He fixed their output on the production report. After setting up a rotation on the two jobs, the workers felt freer. When one worker had a family problem and was unable to concentrate on his work, the other "accelerated" to fill in. In this way, their shared output remained stable. In the individual piecework system, such actions would have been penalized.

Dupont explained their case to the other members of the team by emphasizing the personal problems that had justified the creation of this tandem team.

Several months later, two other workers came forward wishing to follow the example of the two pioneers. The foreman extended his cover for them as well. Two years later, the entire team was working under the new system. This system weakened the customary constraints of the organization. The workers felt less dependent on machinery and output standards. They were also able to make arrangements among themselves, so that "accelerations" could cover for those who had temporary difficulties and worked less efficiently than usual.

For these workers, feeling free and less dependent was an especially valuable attainment. It was the most they could achieve within the confines of a rigid and restrictive organization. To safeguard this freedom, they were prepared to make an effort at their foreman's request. Next, Dupont held discussions with them and spoke to them about his concerns, such as quality of the machined parts, production rate, and absenteeism — i.e., the areas in which supervisors were judged and sanctioned by the corporate hierarchy.

Since he had made an effort to understand the desires of his workers by helping them to work under less restrictive conditions, they responded to him in kind. In this way, his team recaptured high levels of quality and reduced absenteeism.

From that time forward, Dupont felt secure in his relationship with his superiors, who could no longer criticize him. Being ignored was much more gratifying than being censured.

It was in the context of Dupont's tacit agreement with his workers that he made another discovery. The good working ambiance, collective solidarity, and relative freedom that team members enjoyed constituted a powerful motivating factor that enabled the team to achieve financial goals.

By comparing his team with others Dupont noted considerable differences. Once the workers in his team were relieved of certain constraints, they utilized their intellect. The stronger ones compensated for the weakness of the less experienced workers. They shared ideas and used their abilities.

After he discovered this, Dupont made a habit of talking to them about the production schedule. Whenever a new part was to be machined on his production line, he discussed it with his team. His workers took these conversations as a sign of trust on the foreman's part, and they did not hesitate to tell him about potential difficulties or to disclose the existence of unresolved technical problems. Through these exchanges of information and consultations, Dupont was able to avoid the problems that usually worked their way down from the various staff departments (the first level of blockage) to the production units. Whereas errors, omissions, and delays in the departments caused havoc for the other teams, on Dupont's team they were more or less anticipated and therefore reduced.

To an inexperienced observer, this team was no different from the others. The working hours and breaks were regulated everywhere in the same way, and the output and quality standards were the same for each team. Inexperienced eyes did not recognize the factors that distinguished Dupont's team. His workers stayed together during their breaks. Unlike his counterparts, the foreman always remained calm, and from time to time he discussed with two or three workers an unusual or unexpected problem. Whereas the other teams had frequent disputes, Dupont's workers seemed to be on good terms with one another.

These scarcely visible differences evidently revealed no trace of the removal of the piecework output system. Not even Dupont's fellow supervisors guessed the truth.

One of his counterparts, with whom Dupont was on good terms, could never understand his composure. On the day of the production manager's weekly meeting with the supervisors, his hands trembled, and he hid his fear by speaking loudly. He could be heard in every corner of the huge shop room. His nervousness also affected his team.

This foreman, appointed at the same time as Dupont, compared meeting day to the hunting of prey. The paths of retreat cut off, the only opening was guarded by the production manager. His fear turned into aggression, and before his manager even mentioned his name among the poor performers, he went on the offensive by listing all the blunders committed by administrative departments.

Another foreman systematically took sick on the day of the meeting. A third foreman carefully prepared his defense by preparing "written proof" that he had followed orders from upper management.

The free-for-all started as soon as the meeting began. The group of supervisors organized around the production manager was not a skill group like his team. There was no exchange of ideas or mutual assistance. The only talking was in monologues. The manager approached the foremen not to help or understand them but to criticize them. So Dupont kept his ideas to himself.

Labor Organizations Cling to Traditional Structures
(see Figure 3, quadrants 13, 23)

The fact that the labor representatives could not get the better of Raymond Dupont, even though they were successful in other teams, has an explanation. They had their own way of interpreting the different phenomena of the workplace and of representing the employees' expectations. But the foreman was closer to the truth than the labor representatives were. He understood that his workers desired *to be less dependent*. The system he implemented responded directly to their wishes, whereas the wage increases demanded by the unions did not. Of course, no one refused an increase or bonus, but the desire to be less dependent remained as strong as ever.

Unions ultimately specialize in a particular type of explanation or grievance. Like any other group, a union must organize and finance its operation, and it does so according to the same organizational models that company managers themselves use: union groups adhere to a model based on intensive specialization of functions and centralization of responsibilities.

Certain labor groups also cling to a company's old rigid organization, however demotivating it may be. This attachment is reinforced by the high degree of selectivity of the individual abilities that are used in the workplace, which leads to individual and collective dissatisfaction within the confines of the rigid organization. That dissatisfaction is the basis for the grievance-mongering role of the unions.

History has played a role in the process as well. The union movement in France, long unrecognized as a means of employee protection, also had several internal divisions. Several factions created internal competition. Ideological disagreements led to splits, which reinforced the rivalry and one-upmanship among the different union groups.

Throughout its history, therefore, unionism in France has made scattered, conflicting efforts at improving work conditions. But it is doubtful that such conflict is the principal factor in this situation.

In Dupont's company, the conflicting efforts, the confrontation between interests, and the development of negative individualism that arose from the rigid operational structure of the departments and production units prevented them from adapting to the requirements of the competitive market. This negative correlation (Figure 3, quadrants 12, 21) interfered with establishing an individualized organization and with using the employees' internal motivation. Negative individualism continued to impede any evolution.

Conflicting interests existed everywhere — among members of the board of directors, between corporate management and some of its departments, between the sales and production functions, and between the production unit supervisors and line workers. The labor representatives noted these conflicts and, understandably, used them in their own way.

Even in this kind of situation, though, one can always find decision makers or innovators who experiment with ways of creating harmony among various viewpoints and efforts.

Hierarchical Organizations Ignore Expectations

The approach of an innovator runs counter to the logic of a hierarchical organization. The foreman's superiors always began with their own problems, never with the problems of their subordinates. This approach reinforced negative individualism, an avoidance attitude, and a search for security in the supervisory ranks.

Such an approach had no rational basis. If it were applied to technical matters, it would cause serious errors in judgment and analysis. The principal source of mediocre performance in production units was therefore a demotivating hierarchical approach. Its frame of reference was purely financial objectives, rather than the difficulties and disruptions produced by business instability that made life hard for line supervisors.

Dupont managed to break with the type of corporate hierarchical thinking in which objectives are handed down and frontline employees are simply at the service of upper management. Instead, he based his approach and the team's organization on the expectations and inner motivation of his personnel. Team members adopted constructive attitudes, which led to excellent financial performance.

Dupont's approach is illustrated in Figure 9. This diagram shows two phases in the development of Dupont's team. In phase one (1-7), the line supervisor strives to respond to the workers' problems and aspirations; in phase two (8-10), the team gradually accepts the goals set by the supervisor. The skill group constitutes the intersection of these two phases, the point at which the two separate levels are joined into a forum for professional, rather than hierarchical relationships. Phase one was intended to create the conditions for a new motivation, and phase two triggered a change in the old negative attitudes.

Dupont's approach is thus a kind of synthesis, combining two levels often considered antagonistic into a single collaborative unit and uniting them around a single goal. Convergences of this kind are generally hindered by hierarchical divisions in the workplace.

In many cases, moreover, the overall operational structure of companies encourages conflicting efforts and dispersed objectives. The case of Dupont's production manager is revealing in this regard. His extremely hierarchical method of operation created avoidance, defensive attitudes, and aggressiveness in the

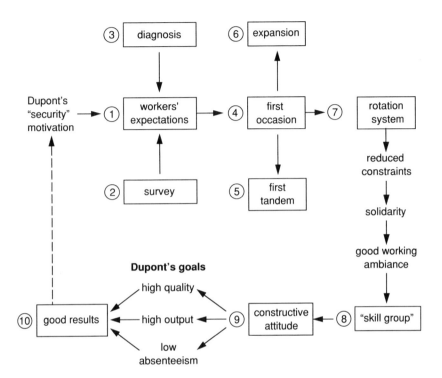

Figure 9.

supervisory ranks. Such a method encourages supervisors to think more about their own security than about work efficiency.

Dupont's approach erased the customary hierarchical boundaries. It was he who approached his workers, accepted their aspirations, and helped them achieve them. Through his help and understanding, solid relationships were established among the team members that were based not on power but rather on reciprocity and on the complementarity of functions and respective skills and abilities.

"I would like to help you to become less dependent and to feel at ease in the team," the foreman said. The workers responded constructively to this appeal and in turn helped the foreman produce satisfactory results. Consequently, their professional relationships were based on skill, ability, and mutual assistance and not on dependence and subordination.

The path that Dupont chose to create these relationships was long. The different stages, grouped into two phases, provide a good illustration. Most managers in a corporate hierarchy, when pressured or incompetent in this area, want to proceed faster than Dupont did. Therefore, they completely abandon the first phase (which is essential for creating ties of reciprocity) and go directly to the last stage (the three goals in the diagram), and then wait for results.

By acting in this manner, however, these supervisors can only partially win the compliance of their workers. When they pressure their subordinates, they demotivate them, cut themselves off from them, and even create feelings of hostility. A considerable number of conflicts are created in this way. Thus, many employees end up investing in obstruction or avoidance — i.e., in negative attitudes.

In rigid organizations, this is the most typical process in the development of negative individualism and demotivation. It is a dangerous process, particularly in the new economic environment, because it inevitably increases unproductive costs and leads to higher prices.

The Determining Variables for Action
(see Figure 4, quadrant 13)

The foreman's extensive analytical ability enabled him to understand the mechanisms governing the formation of attitudes in his team. Obstruction and avoidance represented a negative individualism that was quite typical in the lower levels of the organization and even among the supervisory ranks.

By observing his workers, Dupont came to understand that this negative individualism was not innate but was acquired. Its genesis was intimately related to the working environment and the way in which the work was organized.

Dupont himself was a part of that environment and organization. In the eyes of his workers, he represented the corporate hierarchy. His working style and his relationships with the members of the team could therefore be experienced by the workers either as additional constraints or as an aid in making them feel more independent in their work.

Most of the factors that determined the technical, interpersonal, and organizational environment of the team depended not on him but rather on the technical staff and upper levels of the organization. Nevertheless, there was one variable that he was in control of: his own attitude toward the workers. By varying it, he could create experimental situations and observe the responses. This approach often can be used at the front-line level to test the behavior of the workers.

By observing their reactions, he became aware of the wide variety of individual characteristics in his team. The reaction time varied, moreover, according to the workers' degree of environmental conditioning. Those who had invested their energy in non-work-related occupations responded more slowly than the others.

Dupont also realized that the various factors did not at all have the same degree of importance for different team members. So he had to conduct a strategic analysis of the variables. Through experimental situations, he was able to confirm his hypothesis that the individual output system of work was a determining variable. For the workers, that system of work symbolized nearly all the constraints of the rigid organization.

He ultimately had two significant variables: (1) the team's organization, which was not dependent on him, and (2) his own attitude, which he controlled very well and could vary to test his workers.

His action could not at first be based on the second variable. It could be controlled only after the team made progress and an understanding had been established between him and his workers.

Thus his analysis proceeded. The foreman had an experimental approach. He did not judge team members according to preestablished principles and criteria; instead he tested them in relation to the determining variables.

Once he abandoned the hierarchical attitude (i.e., imposing tasks and penalizing low individual outputs) and replaced it with a helpful attitude, he noted a change in the workers' behavior within a few months. This served as proof ("test result") that his own attitude was a determining variable in creating the substance of their individual behavior. The substance varied according to his own behavior.

The foreman did not, of course, conduct these tests scientifically. The conditions were not at all favorable. He did not select a representative sample, nor did he create a control group or conduct a formal investigation. By taking advantage of the rare openings in the team organization, he nevertheless followed a very effective experimental approach whose stages resembled those used by scientific researchers.

A major difference between the two approaches was that the foreman was part of the environment he was studying. He depended closely on most of the variables and experienced the team's situation profoundly, even emotionally.

Whereas extensive integration in the environment and considerable dependence on the variables can become a handicap, an emotional experience that seriously hampers scientific study, in Dupont's case these circumstances had particular advantages. His strong personality and analytical ability enabled him to adopt a detached attitude in relation to his environment and to his own dependent relationships.

Researchers generally achieve this kind of detachment by nonintegration in the environment in which they conduct their investigations. Clearly, this would not work for the foreman, who had to adapt his approach to environmental variables. He followed and completed his observations and the conclusions drawn from them, giving his approach an intuitive appearance, even though it was, in the end, analytical and strategic.

Using this approach, Dupont identified the variables that created the main blockages in the plant's operational structure. In light of his integration into the environment of the team, he had to circumvent these different blockages in order to succeed.

A Quintessential Blockage:
The Power of the Corporate Hierarchy

In the foreman's company, there were numerous blockage points. Disputes, conflicts of interest, dispersed efforts, and knots of wastefulness and negative individualism developed around these points.

One source of these blockages was hierarchical ambition — that is, the distortion of internal motivation. In fact, in this company, as in many others, the distribution of roles and functions was accompanied by a larger or smaller share of power.

In the production unit where Dupont worked, this was flagrant. The foremen, in groups of three, were under the orders of the head foremen. The head foremen answered to a production unit chief, who in turn worked under the production manager.

This simple organization chart is found in most industrial and business firms, as well as in the service industry. But even beyond the number of successive levels, the distribution of roles was the significant factor in this case.

The foremen handled production itself. The head foremen were in charge of financial management and calculated outputs, quality coefficients, and rejection rates and compared them among the teams. The production unit chief principally handled personnel management — staffing requirements, attendance, replacements, leave, and training. The production manager "supervised" everything, collected the management reports, criticized the teams, and reported the results to the production director.

Financial management is a useful task, as is personnel management. Dupont, for one, liked to know how his team placed in relation to the others, so he needed ratios and coefficients. His problem was that these management functions, which could provide him with useful information, were "above" him in the hierarchy.

Why did these different tasks turn into management powers? Why was the financial management of the production lines higher on the organizational chart than production itself? And why was personnel management placed at a still higher level? Above all, does financial management need more power than production? And must it have less power than personnel management?

The introduction of dependent and subordinate relationships into work relationships by varying the amounts of power accorded to each function quite naturally gave these functions different relative values. Production became less important than financial management, which deferred to personnel management.

But these values — the secondary effects of the power accorded to the different levels within the corporate hierarchy — completely modified the relationships between the functions.

Dupont needed to know financial ratios in order to conduct his activity on the basis of results. He was also interested in the indicators from personnel management, which gave him a fairly accurate view of the attitude of the workers. Accordingly, these two functions (head foreman and production unit chief) were of service to him and complemented his work by providing him with comparative quantified data pertaining to the production unit's activities.

In practice, however, this complementarity disappeared. Complementarity involves mutual assistance, an "osmosis" between roles and information inputs. On the job, however, subordinate relationships, orders, penalties, and criticism were the norm. This was because complementary functions at the same level were set up vertically in a pyramid-shaped organization chart. They were reinforced in that vertical placement by assigning increasing portions of power to the higher levels. The idea of complementarity thus disappeared.

Armed with that power, the foremen went to the head foremen to demand an accounting. They went with figures in hand, not to give the foremen information or consult with them but rather to evaluate them. The same situation happened between the head foremen and the production unit chief, and between the chief and the production manager.

Instead of seeking information, however valuable it might be, the foremen had avoided their superiors or adapted an aggressive attitude to stop their criticism. In some cases, they placed themselves under the protection of a union. In short, functions that could have remained complementary became a source of division, hostility, and demotivation. The internal opposition of these functions encouraged the creation of negative individualism.

In contrast to the negative consequences of the hierarchical relationships of a rigid organization, Raymond Dupont's approach motivated and did not generate negative attitudes.

How did he achieve this result? Instead of imitating his superiors, he positioned himself horizontally in a context of complementary relationships, rather than vertically (using subordinate relationships). In a sense, he "disorganized" his relationships with his team.

These two types of relationships produce diametrically opposed attitudes, which are summarized in Figure 10.

Dupont had few problems and received few inspections, censures, or criticisms because he had the trust and the voluntary contribution of his workers. This enabled him to produce excellent results.

He achieved these results by individualizing the jobs. In effect, his action removed the traditional constraints that were organized around the individual piecework output system and redistributed tasks according to personal potential and abilities. This phase, described in the next chapter, was the most interesting part of Dupont's approach.

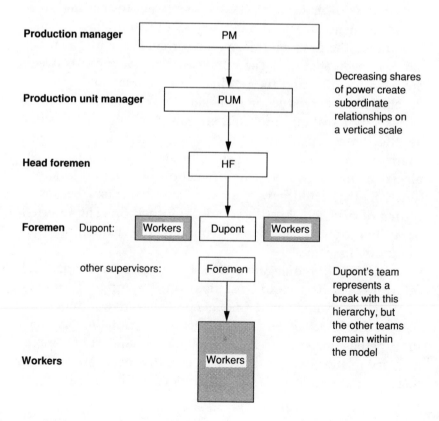

Production manager — PM

Decreasing shares of power create subordinate relationships on a vertical scale

Production unit manager — PUM

Head foremen — HF

Foremen — Dupont: Workers | Dupont | Workers

other supervisors: Foremen

Dupont's team represents a break with this hierarchy, but the other teams remain within the model

Workers — Workers

Figure 10.

———

CHAPTER SIX

Individualizing Jobs Increases Efficiency

An Approach to Individualizing Jobs
(see Figure 4, quadrants 11, 12)

In the absence of a well-thought-out, carefully prepared top-down course of action, Raymond Dupont had to conduct an experiment to liberate jobs from their demotivating constraints.

This experiment enabled the foreman to find openings despite many obstacles. The most important opening, in fact, was the expectations of the members of the team. The corporate hierarchy did not utilize employee expectations as a vehicle for efficiency, and labor representatives interpreted them in a way that led to grievance actions.

The foreman understood that expectations, augmented by dissatisfaction, hid internal motivations that were often stifled and distorted. Penalizing such motivations risked causing conflict. On the other hand, by preparing a setting in which the employees could invest their motivations, it was possible to achieve a great deal of efficiency.

The *penalizing* approach is hierarchical in nature, while the *motivational* approach is used by leaders. Dupont's strategy was based on the latter approach and allowed him to create trusting relationships with the members of his team.

Dupont's approach consisted of a series of stages:

- Taking expectations into account
- Creating relationships of trust
- Eliminating organizational constraints through a collective output system
- Individualizing jobs, making it possible to distribute tasks according to personal potential and abilities
- Setting technical and financial goals in the interest of the company.

In this approach, the fourth stage, individualizing jobs, had strategic value. It was a true turning point that marked a change of attitude among the team members. This stage lasted longer than the preceding ones and required the foreman to thoroughly analyze the personal aptitudes of his workers and the tasks for which the team was responsible. A synthesis of these two aspects made it possible to individualize jobs.

In large firms in the manufacturing and service sectors, the employees generally must adapt to the jobs and their corresponding constraints. Such a situation narrows the field for exercising personal abilities and skills. Under competitive market conditions, it leads clearly to the underemployment of human potential.

For the team, on the other hand, reversing the old principle meant an absolute break with long-standing practice; it challenged the foundation of the rigid operational structure. That foundation on which job specialization was based determined the operation of the plant.

This was obvious in the production units, but it was equally true, although less visible, in the upper levels of management and in the various functional departments.

The functions of these departments were rigorously specialized. Switching roles among departments was out of the question. A design technician in charge of developing modifications requested by customers worked, in essence, according to the output principle. It was out of the question to trust that technician with the overall responsibility for seeing an important modification through to its conclusion. After all, he only did technical design; other departments handled the rest.

Nevertheless, a greater measure of responsibility that did not end at his departmental boundaries would have enabled the design technician to follow and manage the gradual implementation of the modification from start to finish. The technician with an overall perspective of the different phases of the work process would have a better grasp of the source of the misunderstandings and conflicts among the departments and between departments and production units. Consultations with coworkers and even with the machine shop and assembly shop foremen would allow him to take into account any practical and manufacturing problems in his technical design.

Finally, a flexible organization can respond more effectively to the new economic situation than a rigid organizational concept can. In fact, models evolve and change quickly, and it is not easy to update designs in every instance. Small errors and omissions sometimes caused the technician to work on an incomplete or inaccurate design. These inaccuracies gravitated downward to the production units via the designed modification, adding to the usual disagreements.

This was the source of the most frequent misunderstandings between the engineering and production departments. Dupont's reform gave more responsibility to the workers. If there was any doubt about a design prepared by the engineering department, Dupont's workers alerted their foreman, who then went to see the technician in question. In his team, this was a preventive measure. In the other teams, in contrast, the workers executed designs erroneously, even when they knew that the machined parts would be unusable.

Why did this happen? Their job descriptions did not list "observing," "analyzing," "pointing out errors," or "making proposals." Moreover, the qualifications for their jobs involved only psychomotor intelligence — movements coordinated to carry out production steps, which were compensated according to output. Consequently, they did not use other kinds of intelligence. In addition, the system of compensation based on output did not motivate them at all. Therefore, each error that was discovered after the fact represented a heavy loss for the plant.

By ending the individual output system, the foreman opened the way for a motivating organization of work that responded not only to new financial requirements but also to the expectations of the team members. This unified financial and interpersonal goals, internal motivation and tasks.

The Practice of Individualizing Jobs
(see Figure 4, quadrants 11, 12)

The foreman could not conduct studies of abilities and tasks in an official manner because he did not have the authority to do so. He carried out his studies informally and experimentally. Each study was concrete and formed an integral part of the work.

Dupont had one worker in particular who was slow but conscientious and persistent and could approach a technical problem and solve it. This person was continually under pressure within the individual output system. In addition, he was in disfavor with the corporate hierarchy because of his mediocre output and his slowness. He had good qualities, but they were unusable within the context of a rigid organization of work.

As soon as the individual output system had been weakened on the team and other, faster team members were handling a large enough collective output, the foreman entrusted him with difficult pieces that the quick workers didn't like doing. This worker, who had been disliked and often criticized and traumatized by management's censure, showed that he was capable of doing good work and that he could become useful.

A kind of reciprocity became established between him and the other members of the team. The faster ones turned over the experimental prototype or preproduction pieces to him because they required analysis and the detection of unforeseen problems rather than speed. The "slow worker" did them a valuable service because his slowness was not so much a disability but a talent for observation and concentration. These qualities were recognized only when the work load was assigned according to individual abilities and not just according to uniform output standards.

Motivation for Small Improvements
(see Figure 4, quadrant 11)

The new system proved equally effective in another area. The machines were modified and improved from time to time. However, due to the specialization of tasks, the smallest technical change had to be prepared by the engineering department or by the methods department. The foreman filled out a request, his superior verified it, and the production unit chief passed it along to the production manager for his signature. The production manager forwarded it to the department concerned, where the request often went through the same procedure. In view of the number of management levels, this was clearly a slow and costly procedure. Many times the requested change was not implemented until several weeks later.

The foremen did not understand this, since the requested alterations were often trivial. The lengthy official procedure — the embodiment of hierarchical specialization — was entirely comparable to the specialization of the blue-collar jobs. It was broken down into small parts and did not allow the person who originally suggested the change to take overall responsibility for it. Most of the foremen would have liked to defend their ideas and to discuss costs and anticipated savings with the functional departments. Such a procedure, based on a regrouping of responsibility, would have stimulated the requesting party and prompted further thinking about the request and how to present it effectively. It would have developed creative individualism.

In this plant, however, the idea of regrouping the different phases of the machine modification activity was out of the question, for both the production units and the departments. Unfortunately, the manner in which this procedure was fragmented into specialized phases and entrusted to successive levels of the organization demotivated the foremen, creating widespread overloads, bottlenecks, dissatisfaction, and tension.

Dupont's approach created an unheralded breakthrough in this situation. The gradual expansion of the workers' personal aptitudes in the field of application made it possible to set technical and financial goals for the team. But this operational structure required frequent consultations. For this reason, Dupont had to gather the workers together in small group meetings where it was possible to bring up matters such as personal problems, machining schedules, deviations, and disruptions.

These informal meetings, integrated into the work, encouraged workers to exchange interesting comments and ideas. These ideas formed the basis of small improvements that made it possible to enhance collective output and use the time saved for additional exchanges. The team quickly incorporated this unofficial practice into its operations.

These small improvements were an important consequence of job individualization because they signaled the rapid development of a spirit of initiative among the team members. They represented a connection between creative individualism and financial efficiency, two elements that are often directly linked as small improvements stimulate research and even turn into new products.

Dupont knew that a worker who was a handyman could implement small technical changes or improvements without assistance from the technical departments. He realized that this would relieve the departments of subordinate tasks so that they could devote more energy to large-scale innovations.

At the same time, the team members' connection with a technical improvement would stimulate and motivate them to think further and to try more profitable solutions. But despite these advantages, manipulating the specialized roles of the departments and the organizational structure was out of the question because they represented the basis for the plant's operations. The teams were supposed to execute their quantitatively determined schedule; the rest was not supposed to concern them, even if it involved "their" machines. After a few timid trial-and-error attempts with his superiors, Dupont abandoned the idea of an official change of roles, finding it an impossible dream.

In his own system, however, he started an important development. His "slow worker," who was an excellent observer, pointed out potential improvements. They were usually simple and easily implemented and required no investment.

Then, instead of following the customary procedure, he entrusted his "handyman" to implement the improvements. This person, who had been considered superfluous by the quicker members of the team, did an excellent job. He obtained parts through a friend in the storeroom, discussed his problem with appropriate workers in the maintenance department, and developed a revised design.

The output on certain machines improved without further effort. Dupont used this unheralded gain to protect his system still further. The more these small improvements enhanced collective output, the more he could reduce his workers' individual output in order to redistribute tasks according to their inclination, experience, and abilities.

As a result, small improvements and local solutions for small technical problems, which meant greater efficiency and product reliability for the plant, gave Dupont more security and easily ensured good collective output. The workers were no longer tightly and uniformly bound by job constraints and could work according to personal preference.

Individualized Organization Uses
Employee Inquisitiveness
(see Figure 4, quadrant 12)

Another worker on the team who had been criticized often in the past because he made mistakes panicked when problems occurred. So Dupont entrusted him with a stable job that suited his preference, and the man worked with remarkable regularity. He felt more at ease within the team than he had before, and the foreman gained from this situation, as did the plant through him. This employee could focus on work that required great regularity and a high degree of precision and thereby rendered a considerable service to his team.

A third worker, who was not at all as regular as his coworker, was more inquisitive. He was drawn to anything new. If the latest model of a machine was being installed in a neighboring production unit, he looked for any reason to excuse himself to go watch.

This worker was clearly disliked by the corporate management. He had already received several warnings and was on probation. His output was, in fact, irregular, and his absences were interpreted as uncaring and undisciplined.

Inquisitiveness had no place in an individual output system and was not listed in his job description. Nevertheless, it was a valuable internal motivator. Once the team's collective output became large enough, Dupont tried to cover him and use his curiosity. He entrusted him with machining parts that had to be done at the last minute so that the assembly shop could finish an urgent job or when a last-minute replacement had to be made for a part that had been poorly designed by the engineering department.

Whereas these jobs — real wild cards — annoyed most members of the team, the inquisitive worker enjoyed them because they put him in contact with the assembly shops that used his pieces. Not only was he happy to have a work load that matched his inclination and abilities, but the match between his personality and the individually adapted organization of work rendered a valuable service to the team.

Collective Motivation:
The Basis of Professional Relationships
(see Figure 4, quadrant 13)

On the personal level, the main outcome of Dupont's action was that employees worked according to their inclinations and preferences. They did not experience their activities as constraining but, on the contrary, felt useful and motivated. This radical change, brought about by replacing individual piecework with collective output, made it possible to individualize the team's organization of work and change relationships between workers.

Before the experiment, in fact, there were no true professional relationships between the workers. Individual employees were concerned only with their own output. Since output varied from one person to another, and since that inequality created wage disparities, interpersonal relationships were inevitably strained. A tension prevailed between workers in certain positions, and acts of hostility were not unusual. Corporate management maintained that certain workers must be jealous of others' output.

After Dupont's reform, the "jealousy" disappeared. People knew each other better than they had before. They also knew

the service rendered by each person and the respective importance of those services.

In this way, a kind of collective motivation was generated.
The reform not only improved the environment but also
brought about a mutual understanding of services rendered and
a high degree of complementarity in the roles performed. The
change in relationships was profound. Thus, individual output
established by Dupont and his workers could vary slightly,
without risk and without creating hostility or jealousy.

This mutual understanding also created a kind of regrouping
of workers. The team developed several preferred work styles
or interest groups with which members identified themselves.
This was particularly true in the three examples cited above.
The regrouping revealed shared affinities, inclinations, and
interests that resulted in true professional relationships and
even bonds of friendship.

The environment in this team — where each person worked
according to his own skills and abilities and where true professional relationships were formed between workers — was considerably different from the environment in other teams. The
small groups that formed around similar work styles always
went to the cafeteria together. They also had exchanges on the
job when one or another needed advice or assistance.

Dupont's team became a skill group and escaped the mold of
the traditional organizational model.

Developing Creative Individualism
(see Figure 4, quadrant 11)

Dupont's conclusive experiment could, of course, have gone
much further. He reversed the traditional precedence of
machine over worker, which opened up staggering possibilities.

If the plant's management discovered these possibilities, it
would be able to recover a 20 percent loss that burdened the

manufacturing cost so heavily that the company had gone into debt to make the most indispensable investments.

But hardly anyone knew about the team's experiment, and its extremely motivating individualized organization remained informal. The spectacular results occurred on the front lines, which was considered to have the least competent management.

How, then, was it possible to open up this new territory? Because of Dupont's concern for avoiding unpleasant criticism, he aimed for financial goals. To achieve those goals, he needed assistance and collaboration from his workers, so he changed the traditional procedure used in his plant. First *he* became a part of his team members' expectations; a little while later, the two approaches were combined. From then on, any improvement carried out in the interest of his workers (so that the workers would feel at ease in the team and would work according to their abilities) had financial repercussions such as improved collective output, dependable quality for machined parts, and a low level of absenteeism.

The essential action was removing employees' close dependence on machines. This marked the beginning of a constructive attitude and creative individualism that resulted in many positive consequences — collective output, small improvements, and technical innovations.

Employees could work according to their inclinations and abilities, creating a solidarity between the positions on the team. Mutual assistance was a daily occurrence. Another fact was that the sense of responsibility and innovative inclinations were rooted in the small groups formed around the preferred styles of working, because these groups were the means of ensuring that the team had a comfortable collective output.

It was precisely those attitudinal changes by employees in relation to their work that opened the possibility for extensive progress. In fact, everything was built on these new constructive attitudes.

Whereas, on other teams, periodic work interruptions upset the production schedule and conflicts broke out because of job responsibilities, on Dupont's team workers compared their ideas and tried out small innovations so that the team could be relatively autonomous. These were two very different attitudes: one was grievance-based and hostile, and the other constructive.

A kind of "knowledge capital" was accumulating within the team. The small technical modifications and improvements made work more relaxed and more interesting and made it possible to think, observe, and experiment.

None of this was recorded or written on forms because it was completely contrary to the official system of organization. The team's operational structure had to remain informal and officially unrecognized despite its motivating aspect. But this did not stop a kind of collective knowledge from accumulating in the foreman's skill group.

Small-scale Creativity:
A Sign of Highly Motivated Workers
(see Figure 4, quadrants 11, 13)

That collective knowledge was about not only jobs (i.e., machines), but everything connected with collective output. Some members of the team were more inclined toward tinkering and small technical inventions; others had ideas about stocking, tools, materials handling, equipment breakdowns, and quality defects. This small-scale creativity offered great potential for improvements by which, in the end, each person could find the area that best suited his abilities.

Although these different aspects of work were not specifically production tasks, they did in fact play an important role in the collective output. A truck driver furnished the production unit with supplies and cleared the passageways of finished products that had been inspected. Quite often, however, he was overloaded. A member of Dupont's skill group started lending him a hand — something that was never done in the other teams.

Two or three workers who had a particularly reliable sense of measurement were called on by the others if there were doubts about defects. Every machined piece was inspected by the operators, which was an additional guarantee against reprimands from the quality control department.

The plant's quality control department did not examine all the pieces, only the samples. This procedure was sufficient but not completely reliable. Dupont's system compensated for the inadequacy of sampling.

Dupont's group had a young man who had trained as a mechanic but remained with the team due to lack of positions in the maintenance department. As soon as the collective output system provided enough coverage, he could devote himself to addressing minor breakdowns. Whereas the other teams lost a great deal of time with these "trifles" (an annoyance for the maintenance department, which strained relations with the machine shops), on Dupont's team these breakdowns were repaired without delay.

As a result, the foreman's team suffered little from the traditionally poor relationship between production and maintenance. The minor breakdowns were repaired by the group mechanic. Since he never complained about maintenance, Dupont received quick service from that department when there was a major breakdown.

As soon as there was a breakdown on one of the machines, Dupont stopped work on the other machines on the same line. In such instances, the operators involved went spontaneously to help on the other lines or did the supplementary tasks already described.

By using such a flexible distribution of tasks, the machines were not unequally burdened, and there were no delays or premature completions such as those that caused hostility between positions on the other teams. Finally, through this practice, the machines on the three lines were kept in good repair. In the event of a major snag, the other lines could always accelerate to safeguard the team's collective output.

Specialized and Hierarchical Organizations Fragment Efforts
(see Figure 4, quadrants 21, 22, 23)

What was the impact of these activities as they spilled over into areas such as materials handling, inspection of parts, and minor breakdowns?

Dupont and his workers considerably reduced the number of risks in the work. They not only removed risks that gravitated down from the various departments in the form of errors, omissions, and improper technical modifications, but they also reduced the number of risks due to imperfections, the fluctuating work load for materials handling, unsatisfactory quality control, and the waiting time imposed by maintenance.

A numerical comparison between the losses caused by these risks in the other teams and the savings achieved by Dupont's workers would show a gap of 10 to 15 percent in costs.

Some decision makers within the corporate hierarchy are perplexed, and even skeptical, when confronted by such a figure. "Aren't we doing everything possible to remove the risks?" "Isn't the methods department working to reduce downtime?" "Isn't materials handling making an effort?" "Doesn't maintenance have strict orders to repair machine breakdowns immediately?"

Indeed, the operational departments (the plant has five) work to reduce expenses pertaining to the supplementary jobs, which are not directly productive but which nonetheless burden the cost. In fact, the parts must be transported from one production unit to another, samples must be taken to determine the defect rate, and the operations must be timed so that the machines can be "put in charge."

Nevertheless, all of these "supplementary jobs" handled by the different departments are really *new constraints* for those who perform them. In practice, this system of horizontal (functional) specialization operates as a struggle. The functional departments want to eliminate the risks and reduce downtime and implementation time. At the other end of the system, the operators, who play only an executing role are paid according to output, react to this activity with distrust and insubordination. This should not be surprising. Don't these departments want to nibble away at their time and increase their output? Don't they want to do everything possible to increase the pace of production work? Therefore, the operators oppose such actions.

The struggle and the mutual distrust are burdened considerably by a job description system of compensation. In Dupont's plant, that system was determined by the principle of individual output. Compensation was given for direct, performance-based output. This means that, if someone made an additional effort in the area of supplementary jobs not included in the job description, that effort did not count toward wages, regardless of how deserving it was. Employees refused these minor but useful jobs because they interfered in good direct output.

This attitude was inherent in the specialization of jobs and was appropriate for the long, prosperous period in which the primary criterion in manufacturing was productivity, which imposed external motivations on the employees.

But that system became blocked periodically because the persons performing the production steps did not accept time compression. They slowed down when their operations were timed, and they demanded that job descriptions be revised when there were "unstipulated tasks." There was antagonism between internal motivation (desire to work according to one's abilities) and external motivation (discipline imposed by the constraints of job specialization).

All of these things were experienced as a struggle or a conflict. The administrative departments felt qualified to impose changes in production time on the operators, and the workers did everything possible to thwart those efforts. It was a fruitless struggle, filled with conflicting efforts and demotivation. But these costly conflicts were not yet dangerous during this golden period, when companies enjoyed a comfortable level of overall profitability.

Activities Spill Over into Operational Functions
(see Figure 4, quadrants 11, 12)

It is an old story. For many decades, the machines were put in charge. They were timed, and the operators were there only to carry out what was required of the machines.

This thinking was reversed by Dupont's team. The difference was scarcely visible from the outside, but it was enormous. For Dupont's workers, the elimination of downtime, waiting time, and various risks meant that there was more potential for ensuring a comfortable collective output. As collective output went up (although, as a precaution, the team did not exceed a certain limit), the individuals felt freer from the constraints that were created by the operational departments and the individual output system of work.

In this team, the workers, much more than the machines, were "put in charge" on the basis of their abilities and experience. This was the opposite of the old system. It allowed each person to use his potential and ability. Despite all expectations to the contrary, the system was much more efficient than the one that still governed the other teams.

The proof of this was that, while the team had a good collective output (and consequently, good individual outputs), it also performed supplementary jobs to facilitate the individual workers' tasks. Because of a significant organizational transformation, the team's internal motivation was unleashed, resulting in interpersonal harmony and a good financial return.

If the plant's management had taken the work method applied by Dupont a little further, it would have been possible to prevent most of the direct interventions by the methods, quality control, engineering, and maintenance departments. Interventions would have been limited to major problems or technical assistance.

The conflict-filled relationships would have turned into focused efforts and mutual assistance, as shown in Figure 11. This convergence of efforts within Dupont's team was based entirely on a change in motivation and on the rapid development of a creative attitude.

Although there still existed a more or less conflict-filled relationship between the functional departments and the other teams, Dupont's skill group had a kind of complementarity with them. For his workers, entering the domain formerly held exclusively by these departments was a way of eliminating minor obstacles to achieve a good collective output.

What savings were achieved by this method of work? Clearly, no one knew the answer, since no accounts were kept of the unproductive costs that resulted from employees' demotivation, from their conflict-based relations, and from the lack of initiative and innovation in the other teams.

In addition, Dupont's workers assumed these minor responsibilities and implemented these small improvements better than the functional departments did.

Having responsibility for these small jobs was not at all interesting to the various departments. For them, it just meant performing tasks that carried the risk of creating conflict with the machining teams. Does one willingly do time studies, or divide operations by job, or analyze handling procedures, knowing in

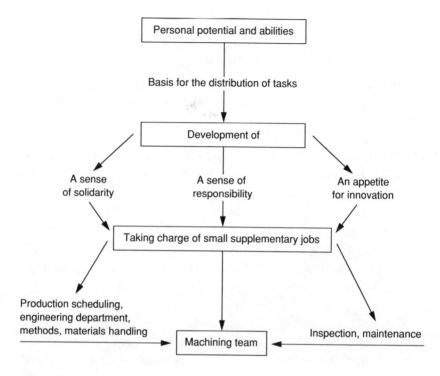

Figure 11.

advance that the outcome will be conflict between the department in question and the teams?

At any rate, they never saw the direct results of such work. All of these odd jobs or "trivia" could hold real interest only for those who were directly concerned. For technicians from the engineering or methods department, they meant nothing.

Activities Spill Over into Management Functions
(see Figure 4, quadrants 11, 12)

Was the system implemented by Dupont expandable? In fact, if it had been expanded to the other teams, it could have absorbed most of the small jobs that burdened the various departments.

The new method had a dual advantage. The team members could have broad responsibility if they did most of the jobs necessary for machining and the operational departments could concentrate on very motivating large-scale problems.

Was it profitable to busy the technicians in the design and methods departments with small technical modifications and risk studies? Even though major modifications and large-scale innovations awaited, there was not enough time for them.

In the system used by Dupont's team, there was a significant possibility of recovering 20 percent of unproductive costs.

From the standpoint of the organization of work, the essential aspects of this system were the removal of the excesses of intensive hierarchical and functional specialization, and the full utilization of the employees' internal motivation.

The team members tended to "regain" the tasks that normally should have been part of their own work load but were separated from it because of the specialization of jobs and functions. This tendency was a sign of their motivation. The workers *wanted* to have full responsibility. They wanted to create, not perform isolated production steps.

Evidently regaining responsibility could not be complete; the team's environment posed a barrier to such an attempt. Nevertheless, the possibilities opened up by the experiment were immense.

Dupont's workers, heartened by a good collective output, could have assumed most of the small jobs given to the various operational departments within the context of specialization of tasks. In that case, the hierarchical specialization might also have lost a considerable part of the rationale for its existence. Weren't the three levels of management above the foremen concerned with these same risks? Didn't they settle problems individually with the various departments? Didn't the head foreman go in person to request service when there was a breakdown? Wasn't it the production manager who tried to solve the scheduling problems with the department concerned?

Dupont had little need for their assistance. His team's operation was flexible enough to accept a change in the machining schedule in emergency situations with no significant loss, while the other teams did not like such changes at all. His skill group adhered to market criteria, while the other teams remained attached to their constraints, which principally related to individual outputs.

Harmony Among Various Types of Motivation

As a skill group, Dupont's team developed a new orientation. The workers were given priority over customary procedures, which reduced their role to performing specialized tasks on machines. Under this new priority their attitudes and motivation became constructive.

Professional motivation — scarce in the other teams — emerged. What motivation can one find in a standardized organization that stifles personal potential and abilities?

In this environment, workers relied on wages (whose effects did not last long), a little camaraderie, and bonds outside of work to create a more pleasant atmosphere.

For Dupont's workers, such non-work-related motivations played a limited role. They did exist, of course, but they were complementary in this network of close ties born out of solidarity on the job.

Wages lost their customary sense of motivation. Moreover, Dupont's workers earned a little more than they did in the old system, since their collective output steadily improved.

The team did not feel completely unanimous about the change in operational structure. Three operators out of twenty were not fully integrated into the new system. They remained on their machines more than the others, moved around less, and expressed fewer ideas than their coworkers. They were assimilated into the good atmosphere, but they didn't seem to have distinctive abilities that could be directly applied in the redistribution of roles.

On another team, the same workers would have become outsiders — people with chronic absenteeism, who play hide-and-seek to escape the managers, or who habitually "call in sick." These workers are moved from one team to another or have dismissal actions taken against them when the possibilities for change have been exhausted.

On Dupont's team, the three men were drawn into the environment and the activity of the other team members, for whom they even performed small services. Their role stopped there, however.

But for the other team members, motivation for work changed a great deal. It consisted of, first, each person's internal motivation, and then a collective motivation (solidarity and morale), and even non-work-related motivations shared by certain team members. These different types of motivation complemented one another harmoniously.

CHAPTER SEVEN

Creative Individualism and the Future

Ending Resistance to Change
(see Figure 4, quadrant 13)

Raymond Dupont's skill group could have prepared the whole plant for the future. Rapid technological transformation of the manufacturing equipment had already guaranteed that evolution would take place. Technological progress had not yet made great headway in this plant, due to the lack of investment capital, but one can nevertheless imagine, on the basis of a few specific local changes, the magnitude of the upheavals that such a transformation would inevitably cause. The old manual trades were facing radical transformation, just as electronic typewriters and word processors have transformed administrative work in offices.

The plant's management could have based its plans and projections on Dupont's and the other innovators' experiences. Ultimately, what was most important was that this team, in contrast to the others, quickly, and without resistance, adapted to technological change.

The upheaval looming on the horizon required serious preparation if resistance to change and serious labor conflict were to be avoided. In fact, the long-standing rigid organization, based on rigorously specialized jobs, had a profound conditioning effect on employees. After ten, fifteen, or twenty years, an employee can lose part of his ability to adapt, and imposing the slightest change will cause him to react with fear or hostility.

In Dupont's team, however, the logic of the old rigid organization had been reversed; his workers had become flexible and versatile. They performed a variety of operations, busied themselves particularly in areas in which they had personal abilities, and encroached on the territory of the operational departments.

These employees were not afraid of change. They even hoped for it because it enabled them to increase their collective output. They became inquisitive. They used different aspects of their intelligence, observed the risks, exchanged observations among themselves, tested hypothetical theories, and implemented small innovations. In short, they changed.

All of those changes were closely aligned with the direction of inevitable technological changes. In view of the electronic revolution and growing competition, it was possible to foresee a genuine upheaval that, in the fairly near future, would completely transform the production system and the roles of employees. The team was preparing for the inevitable future transformation.

A new generation of machines and equipment was settling in to coexist with the old one. These pieces of equipment had already appeared in certain parts of the plant, but they were still an exception and were not well assimilated into the production units. People regarded them with curiosity and distrust.

Growing in Harmony with Technological Change
(see Figure 3, quadrant 22)

In the assembly shop, certain delicate operations requiring a high degree of reliability (because they determined the quality of the final product) had to be automated. There was already an experimental automated section on one assembly line. But it was necessary for a worker to monitor this passage, note any anomalies, observe the slightest signs of malfunctions, and discuss these things with the inspection team. Pure psychomotor intelligence — "doing the job" — was inadequate for this role; other forms of intelligence were required.

This job threw the job classification department into confusion. The department wanted to describe it according to custom and long-standing criteria. They tried to pigeonhole the new job using the old classification system, but the job did not lend itself at all to such manipulation. The tasks were irregular and required no physical effort. Instead, they demanded sustained attention, a sense of responsibility, observation and analysis skills, good relations with the various departments, and a talent for expression and explanation. All of these were individual qualities and criteria that were ignored in traditional assembly jobs.

The situation baffled the operator who monitored the automated section. Before, he used only his psychomotor intelligence; he simply did the manual work that was required by the job.

Those who had to supervise the job — i.e., upper management and the various departments — were also perplexed. In the context of the old rigid organization, job functions were clear and fit perfectly in place. It was they, not the operators, who observed anomalies, noted risks, and experimented with technical solutions.

In the new job, however, the operator had to perform these tasks. What should these other parties do then? Was there any need for intervention by upper management? Would the operator have to transmit his observations to them so they could assume responsibility for the rest?

Because habits die hard, the latter is what in fact happened: management assumed responsibility for making decisions, and the operator's role was reduced to nothing. This role substitution was expensive, however, because it prolonged waiting time when there was a breakdown.

Within the plant, then, people reacted to the idea of a completely new job in the traditional way. It was, moreover, a genuine reflex. No one saw the danger in that reaction, but it was a sign that problems would appear when the new generation of equipment was installed in most of the production units some years later.

This time, technological change, accelerated by increased competition, required changing roles, expanding responsibilities at the front lines of the organization, employing all forms of intelligence, reducing the corporate hierarchy to the absolute minimum, and overlapping between the new jobs and the various departments involved. In other words, it required implementing the employees' creative individualism.

Dupont's skill group already anticipated these needs, which questioned the system of dual specialization (hierarchical and functional) and heralded the future disappearance of the old rigid organization.

This upheaval was also foreshadowed in other production units, although more modestly. In the sheet rolling mill, in addition to the conventional presses that performed only a few production steps, there were already two numerically controlled presses that made it easy to imagine what that production unit probably would look like a decade later.

The old presses were prepared by set-up workers or, in the event of a quick model change, by the operators themselves. It was strictly manual labor. The workers, in groups of two, positioned and then removed the cut sheets at a regular pace.

The new presses, used for large, complex jobs, were preprogrammed, thus eliminating the old production steps. There were other steps, however, such as preparing the schedule according to the sales projections, inspecting the cut pieces, noting the slightest anomalies and analyzing them, and maintaining the two presses.

The sheet rolling mill also had a small machine that ran in accordance with a particular program for "specialized devices," i.e., those designed to customers' specifications. It had a better output than the old equipment and was run by a single operator. His job was to read the technical drawing and program the machine. The small steel sheets, cut to measure, came out a few moments later. He inspected them, noted any defects, and then went to discuss them with the assembly shop — all roles that did not exist on the old machines.

Did the operator need to entrust these roles to upper management and the quality control department? This was, in fact, what they wanted, but they had to forgo the idea because, in this instance, the job would have lost the rationale for its existence.

This was not a routine operator job, i.e., an execution job, devoid of responsibility. The corporate hierarchy was perplexed: if there aren't any operator jobs, then managers become operators themselves. On the other hand, if the operator jobs are modified and the operators assume overall responsibility out of technical necessity, then what will their former managers do?

The dilemma was ignored for the time being. Since there was only one new machine, the issue could be avoided. But for how long?

The same question had already come up and been analyzed and solved in Dupont's team. His team had no need for the customary interventions by the upper ranks or the operational departments. For his workers, technological upheavals posed no unknown threat.

Furthermore, a machine was already operating experimentally in the machine shop. The group's inquisitive worker, who always found reasons to watch it operate, talked about it with his coworkers. They therefore knew that the new machine was highly automated, that it ran on a preset program, and that, by itself, it was capable of producing half the output of a complete line. They were aware that it needed only two or three operators to keep it supplied, monitor it, observe its operation, take samples for inspection, and show the results in graphs, which they discussed with quality control. A traditional line with four specialized machines required eight people.

Dupont's workers, who were not strictly wedded to their jobs, felt very much at ease doing the supplementary jobs, which were just what was needed by the new experimental equipment. It operated under the supervision of the technicians until its permanent installation.

Who would take the new jobs? Dupont's workers were prepared to take them because they were no longer accustomed to working according to the individual output system that the new equipment abolished. They were prepared as well because the team spirit needed for the new positions was highly developed in their group. For them, the difference would not have been significant. They would have had a greater number of supplementary jobs, and they would no longer work directly on machines as they had before.

Creating New Relationships with Machines
(see Figure 3, quadrant 22)

This last point — creating new relationships with machines — required the greatest adaptation. Although several members of the team already spent as much time on small improvements as they did on the machines, a complete separation from the machines would have been felt for a very long time. It was not simply a matter of developing a certain type of ancillary work, a kind of work that was not directly productive. A complete separation from operating machines and the elimination of manual labor — the archetype of shaping metal and of creation — meant for these workers a break with a century of tradition. It meant the disappearance of a trade that, despite its narrow limitations and the intensive specialization of operations, retained a creative aspect because it contributed to the transformation of metal into a useful component so that a final product could exist and function.

The arrival of a new generation of machines eliminated that direct, material contribution, and with the disappearance of the trade, a long history and a long working-class tradition would probably disappear.

Should they regret this disappearance? The question did not arise in those terms. Workers in the production units did not philosophize. They lived the moments of their work. They endured many barriers that prevented them from giving themselves freely to their tasks. They endured constraints that compelled them to cheat, to slow down, and to thwart the timing of operations.

In small enclaves such as Dupont's team, the workers felt free to call on their abilities instead of restricting their input only to psychomotor intelligence. Nevertheless, even for Dupont's workers, their trade and their tradition meant a way of life, a certain social awareness. All of their usefulness and the entire rationale for their work were tied to their contribution to the shaping of metal.

What would remain of all that when direct contact with metal eventually disappeared? Would they still be "workers"?

What would be left of the rules? And the old wages and benefits? What about the hierarchical differences that were so minutely defined?

Eliminating the Middleman
(see Figure 3, quadrants 22, 23)

No one had yet raised such questions in Dupont's plant. The foreman himself would have been surprised to know that, in the not-so-distant future, he would no longer be stifled by three levels of management. He would have been surprised that his principal task would be to coordinate the various types of servicing so that the machines could yield their full output.

No one knew that this new age on the horizon specifically needed more Duponts — more inquisitive, inventive, intelligent people.

Would the workers of the future, with broad responsibility for their work, allow themselves to be represented by elected spokesmen and their ideologies? Would they allow their opinions and expectations to be interpreted by go-betweens from labor organizations, even though the intermediaries in the corporate hierarchy would have disappeared?

That question had not come up because plant management was preoccupied with the present. This was true, even with competitors who were more aggressive than ever, even with costs that, outside the small enclaves, were too high to be truly competitive, and even with management's renewed attempts to breathe new life into the plant.

Those endless efforts were certainly praiseworthy, but they were not very effective because they were aimed principally at immediate, localized improvements. The improvements, instead of reversing the negative trend, risked reinforcing it. Evidence of this could be found, in particular, in the multiplication of organizations designed to coordinate functions that did not get along well or that had conflicting interests.

These intermediary organizations were sometimes inserted hierarchically on the organization chart as an additional level of management. Whenever new tasks appeared, there was a tendency to specialize them according to the traditional logic of the rigid organization. Since new jobs had to be integrated into an existing organizational structure, this tendency gave rise to a gradual expansion of the number of levels of management.

This was nothing new, but the process accelerated with small-scale production and customized products. For this reason, the teams were organized in four levels, of which the lowest one — Dupont's level — was practically devoid of responsibility. The only responsibility still held by that level was production, or rather, the *execution* of production; anything related to risks, exceptions, or malfunctions was handled at higher management levels.

Dupont's team, which solved its own problems and regained the supplementary jobs that were complementary to production, obviously went against that accelerated trend. This was equally true with respect to horizontal intermediaries, whose appointment multiplied the number of phases in the work process. Rapid-fire technological innovations and a significant reduction in the service life of models required the reverse — fewer phases, fewer spokesmen, more overlapping of functions, broader personal responsibility, and full use of individual abilities.

What was the explanation for the appearance of these increasingly numerous middlemen who stifled creative individualism? Creating the positions seemed to be a quick solution when two corporate offices or two departments were unable to cooperate and agree. For this reason, a committee was formed between the sales and technical offices, and a coordinating organization was established between the technical office and production. And for the same reason, a special department rounded out the production process by temporarily setting itself up between the production and the engineering departments for the purpose of assisting them in completing anticipated technical improvements.

These intermediaries quickly became additional links or new phases in the work process.

In short, a new economy, which demanded faster responses, analysis, and reactions than in the past, clashed with the growing complexity of the plant's operational structure. A new economy, which called for the reduction of unproductive costs, clashed with the successive establishment of middlemen who formed the nucleus of an increasing excess in staffing. These were two contradictory and antagonistic tendencies.

The new economy did not require implementing these means of contriving short-lived efficiency but instead reversing the old tendency, as Dupont's team and other small enclaves had already attempted. Unfortunately, those groups, which didn't have problems, did not interest the decision makers, who devoted most of their time to rescue and fix-it activities.

Other teams did not follow Dupont's innovation, and individualized organization, which unleashes each person's internal motivation, therefore could not be generally applied in the production units.

PART THREE

Transferring Management Powers to the Front Lines

Raymond Dupont's actions released the team's jobs from the principal traditional constraints, but he was unable to motivate his workers to the fullest extent possible. The team members definitely appropriated functional and hierarchical powers, but they could not do so legally because the official organization stood in the way.

Small companies have fewer, and less difficult, obstacles to overcome. They have generally no more than three levels of management hierarchy, and these usually involve only a few small departments.

In contrast, in large companies in the manufacturing and service industries, authority and responsibility are distributed in a strictly specialized manner. The various phases of the work process are entrusted to departments and corporate administrative offices. A highly complex management structure, sometimes reaching eight or more successive levels, evolves. Finally, the various areas of personnel management, which comprise the union and labor relations functions, are entrusted to specialized divisions of the human resources office.

Such a rigid organization can be efficient during a stable economic period in which production must remain constant. But inevitably, it experiences serious dysfunctions when stability disappears and when the growth becomes qualitative, as is the case with the competitive market that has developed, particularly since the early 1970s.

Companies generally respond in one of two ways to ongoing technological and economic change. The majority try to use remedial means to make a rigid operational structure more flexible. In contrast, companies freed from old organizational principles undertake experiments to break with tradition and adapt their operational structure to new competitive conditions.

There is a great difference between these two approaches:

- One endeavors to respond to new problems by using old methods, which are quantitative and comprehensive in nature (implementation of remedial mechanisms)
- The other gradually abandons the specialized, rigid operational structure (implementation of an individualized organization).

The individualization of the latter approach requires the removal of traditional job constraints and the transfer of de facto authority and responsibility to the front lines of the organization and the supervisory level. It represents a genuine break with the principle of specialization, the basis for a rigid, Tayloristic organization.

The remedial approach is often used because it seems to offer a quick solution to the problems without upsetting customs and operational mechanisms. If competition requires higher quality in the finished products, then quality control can be intensified. Products are screened for defects twice or even three times in succession, rather than adapting operators' jobs to the quality criterion.

This remedial approach can prove effective in the short term, but it also has serious drawbacks. It does not eliminate the causes of defects, it does not motivate the employees at the lower levels of the organization, and it runs the risk of creating small but wasteful redundancies, which are dangerous under competitive conditions.

The second approach, that of individualizing the organization of work, is much more complex. It requires patient experimentation and a change in behaviors and attitudes. It also runs the risk of generating resistance to change, especially during the second phase, in which de facto authority and responsibility are transferred to lower levels in the organization.

Implementing creative individualism presupposes complementary professional relationships, not dependency. It requires distributing tasks based on individual potential and abilities. It also requires a realistic and functional assignment of duties and responsibilities that make it possible to formulate tasks and to control and monitor output.

Such an individualized organization questions the fundamental principles of a rigid operational structure. It significantly modifies the traditional distribution of functions and replaces hierarchical power with complementary responsibilities.

Because of the extensive nature of the change, it is preferable to work on a modest scale, especially at the beginning. Such an experimental approach is entirely possible through the computerization of process control and data. This is why large companies in the manufacturing and service sectors "subsidiarize" and "departmentalize" their offices and production units. Creating highly autonomous facilities (in which the central offices play only an informational role) whose staffs usually number 100 to 600 employees makes conditions more favorable for individualizing the organization of work.

Such a profound transformation may be mandated despite managerial and administrative resistance due to the imperatives of a competitive market. Banks and insurance companies have already reconfigured functional authority and responsibility to create "special windows" where customers may resolve various problems instead of being given the customary runaround from department to department.

Even government is following suit. Relations between service recipients and staff are being personalized. Economic necessity, rather than pure Cartesian logic, is prompting regional government agencies to regroup previously scattered powers and responsibilities of business-related programs and procedures. Considerable delays caused by dispersed and fragmented responsibilities had resulted in lost orders and business failures, with a corresponding increase in unemployment.

The unsaturated market had no need for powers and responsibilities to be transferred to the lower levels of the organization, since the business environment was stable and production was constant. In contrast, the competitive market requires personal initiative and the implementation of creative individualism. Accordingly, it is necessary to individualize the organization of work by eliminating traditional job constraints and by regrouping duties and responsibilities in instances where practical problems arise.

Raymond Dupont's plant finally acknowledged that need. A developmental plan was prepared on the basis of Dupont's successful experiment, and management decided to replicate it throughout the plant. At the same time, in preparation for the second stage in the development of creative individualism, management granted gradual, extensive autonomy to the various production areas.

These two complementary actions significantly increased the motivation for work in all of the teams, enabling the plant to adapt to the many disturbances caused by the competitive market.

CHAPTER EIGHT

Adapting Organizations to Individual Potential and Abilities

Ineffective Remedies for Blocked Change

Many companies, particularly large and medium-sized ones, hesitate to move toward individualizing jobs and functions because their managers fear anarchy and "bungling." This was the case for a long time in the foreman's plant as well. Indeed, the old well-honed rigid organization imposed a certain discipline, a kind of external motivation.

Can that discipline be replaced with something else, such as internal motivation or freely accepted discipline? And would that be more efficient than the old system? Would decentralization of authority and responsibility permit the calculation of team work loads, job qualifications, and compensation, as the previous system had?

The small localized experiments made it possible to answer these questions and allay such fears. Raymond Dupont's team illustrates that individualization of jobs and work loads releases previously stifled internal motivation, thereby creating much better "discipline" than that formerly imposed on employees.

Since that team's successful experiment, classification has a new meaning. In fact, it is the *workers* who are classified, not the jobs. Mobility, rotation, supplementary jobs, and small improvement activities cause team members to get to know one another quite well. As a result, they concede that one member is "worth more" than another because he contributes more to collective efficiency.

Wages, when based on collective output, can therefore vary according to the immediate value of services rendered, the ideas originated, or the number of small innovations introduced. It is not a rigid system. Less inventive employees can advance and catch up to the others, at least momentarily.

But such a working group, which resolves most of its problems without recourse to upper management and which takes a bite out of administrative and management prerogatives, becomes very demanding. It definitely needs advice and information, but it no longer needs traditional analyses of jobs and work loads or representatives and labor organizations to negotiate its wage scales.

The foreman's team thus represents a radical change, albeit an isolated one. This radical aspect often alarms company managers, who, because they fear that the organization will skid out of control, prefer a "remedial" approach to fundamental change.

Remedial measures appear to promise a quick solution without upheavals. But the overwhelming majority of companies in the manufacturing and service industries already have a long record of experience with remedial solutions. Such solutions are nothing new. They existed even during the long period of high growth.

In brief, there are two types of remedial solutions, depending on the nature of the market. The unsaturated market was marked by a significant increase in wages and benefits, which were employed as a remedy (Figure 3, quadrant 13). In fact, the specialized, rigid organization resulted in a feeling of general dissatisfaction and the development of negative individualism, which was the basis for all kinds of conflicts and various labor grievances.

The end of the unsaturated market and the rapid growth of competition marked the coming of the era of the organizational remedy (Figure 3, quadrant 23), which appeared wherever company operations did not match competitive requirements.

This trend prompted costly methods of individual resourcefulness to circumvent illogical rules. Rapid solutions were sought, without weighing the consequent risk of increasing unproductive costs and creating small hidden wastes and redundancies. The idea was to find a legitimate "gimmick" that would appropriately eliminate a problem without creating future problems. Keeping a small reserve inventory would be seen as a clever device rather than an additional cost to the plant. Inflating the staff while manipulating the work load will be seen as a skillful way of responding to unforeseen circumstances and not as a burden on costs.

In Dupont's plant, there were numerous telltale signs that remedial means were proliferating:

- The implementation of intermediary organizations or buffers
- A rapid expansion of the corporate hierarchy's arbitration and settlement role
- An increase in redundancy
- The flourishing non-work-related relationships and interests to compensate for stifling compartmentalization
- The institution of "unblocking meetings" to study and resolve tricky problems.

In practice, these developments were barely perceptible. Because the sales office wished to call the shots for production, they did not get along well, and a buffer was inserted between them. This consisted of a small committee intended to soften the blows and translate interchanges into acceptable language. This practice reduced the number of misunderstandings and resulted in a certain amount of progress. It was relatively effective in keeping the opponents at arm's length, but such an intermediary body inevitably prolonged actual job deadlines. In addition, it also represented a minor instance of overstaffing.

In the parts of the organization where there were no buffer committees, the managers' arbitration and reconciliation role gained considerably in importance. This was useful because, as disagreements were settled, situations became unblocked. The unblocking was only temporary, however, because the source of the disagreements — horizontal specialization and its consequent structural compartmentalization — was not eliminated.

In short, the pressure of the economic situation required constant removal of obstacles and bottlenecks. Although this process was more or less effective, it did not prevent the formation of new blockages. In addition, the upper levels of management turned into arbitrators.

The habit quickly took hold. As a result, a large number of decision makers in the plant spent a significant part of their time on settlement and arbitration activities. But since those activities did not eliminate operational problems, they had to be constantly repeated. It was a wearying process, and weariness is demotivating. It also creates negative attitudes and compels employees to seek interests outside of their jobs.

Once the habits had taken hold, upper management gravitated more and more often to the lower levels of the organization to settle disagreements and resolve ongoing problems. Generally speaking, the entire corporate hierarchy was "sliding" downward. The consequences of this sliding included hastily adopted measures and inadequately formulated decisions. As a result, new technical and marketing problems arose.

Subsequently, this "semi-open" situation, with its temporary unblockings followed by obstructions, necessarily required clever tactics at the lower levels of the organization. If a supervisor does not want to expose himself to negative criticism, he will try to prevent problems.

There are, however, differing methods for prevention. The methods Raymond Dupont developed were realistic and effective, whereas most of the methods used by his colleagues were nothing more than compromises, sometimes costly ones.

To cope with badly formulated technical modifications, the production unit managers took on additional staff. It was an easy thing to do. This was, of course, a hidden increase that made it possible to use a small group of assemblers for reworking defective products and another group for machining pieces when the technical modifications were improperly devised by the design department.

Given that there was no link of responsibility between the sales/production scheduling department and the warehouse, separated as they were by rigid departmental boundaries, purchasing activities occurred in fits and starts. The production units therefore built up small reserve stocks to avoid scenes with management.

Relationships outside the job in the plant's cultural and sports clubs experienced an extra surge because they represented a valuable source of information. Official information could not be obtained quickly because of the slowness of the organizational structure. Instead it was often obtained through these relationships, which bypassed official channels.

What was the cost of the buffer committees? And of the increase in the arbitration roles? The downward slide of the corporate hierarchy? The rework groups? The back-up inventories?

Since these expenditures were not documented in the accounting system, it was difficult to compute them. However, it was clear that the cost quickly became disadvantageous in relation to the production costs of competitors. In fact, one of the most representative characteristics of the remedial system was communication, i.e., the various means used to transmit and receive messages. Indeed, the proliferation of administrative, management, and labor organization intermediaries complicated and slowed down communication. To perceive this, one needed only to look at the organization chart to find the blockage points, where misunderstandings arose, disagreements lingered, and tension marred the work environment.

There was a close correlation between these remedial phenomena and the blockages. The methods used to eliminate the misunderstandings and remove the blockages were arbitration, separation of opponents by buffer committees, and meetings.

The people invited to such meetings were those who occupied the blockage points, i.e., managerial and administrative decision makers. It was practically never those who performed the actual work in the departments and production units. The problems concerned the workers directly, but it was the intermediaries who "resolved" the problems and subsequently communicated decisions to them.

That communication procedure strangely resembled the buffer role of the committees and the arbitration role of certain members of management.

The drawback is that, in such instances, the communication and the decision take on different appearances; they metamorphose and become criticism or orders. Although economic pressure demanded a mobilization of efforts and the resolution of practical problems on the front lines of the organization, the means of communication and decision making demotivated employees and their direct supervisors.

Eliminating Blockages Unleashes Creative Individualism
(see Figure 4, quadrant 21)

The delay in discovering Raymond Dupont's actions had beneficial effects. Faith in the value of the customary remedial means had been shaken. People began to admit that it was necessary to escape and avoid blockages altogether instead of simply "managing" them.

Before acknowledging that they finally had the solution, however, the plant's decision makers tried to apply imported means and methods of action, without asking themselves whether the nature of those methods was responsive to the problems emerging in the offices, departments, and production units.

They did transactional analyses and tried to create quality control circles in the assembly shop. They attempted to enrich jobs in one department, and they wanted to use employee views as a means of redressing problems. But they installed these methods as if they were doing an organ transplant, without altering the organizational system itself. They assumed that they could achieve spectacular results that met the competitive market imperatives, without, at the same time, creating the conditions necessary to facilitate implementation of such imported methods.

That was why they got no results. Training periods and new initiatives were certainly not useless, but it is unreasonable to hope that these methods and means of action could resolve the problems regarding division of responsibility and cooperation among departments. Neither could they eliminate structural compartmentalization, or create a high degree of motivation while retaining job specialization and a hierarchical structure in work relationships.*

One study revealed that contradiction. For several weeks, investigators noted the most typical blockages, as well as the remedial means used to temporarily remove them (see Figure 12). These blockages were counted and pinpointed on the organization chart. Coded "values" revealed their respective significance.

---

* These various theories and operational methods can be effective if they are used under favorable conditions. But if such conditions are not created beforehand, they lose most of their effectiveness.

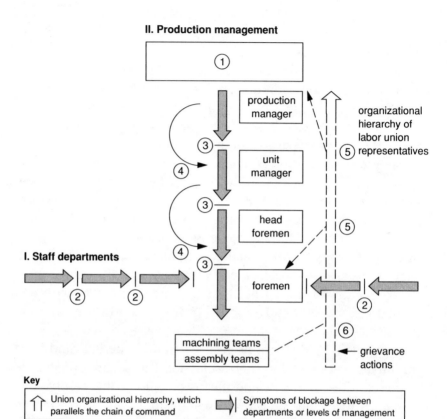

II. Production management

I. Staff departments

Key

| ⇧ Union organizational hierarchy, which parallels the chain of command | ⇨ Symptoms of blockage between departments or levels of management |

1. Product blockage: Technological lead time for product
2. Horizontal blockages: Compartmentalization of departments
3. Specialization of the upper levels of management in problem resolution, due to compartmentalization of departments
4. "Sliding" downward of upper levels of management (institutionalization of the remedial role)
5. Remedial role of labor union representatives
6. Grievance actions due to the inflexibility of the rigid organization and the "management" of problems

I. Horizontal specialization, compartmentalizing the various phases of the work process
II. Vertical specialization of the hierarchical levels of management in the remedial resolution of problems

Figure 12.

The blockages identified actually represented an organized network. This network coincided exactly with the places where there were visible consequences of the extreme specialization of jobs and functions, where most of the remedial means were also applied. Thus, there was a strong correlation between the remedial means and costly blockages.

The principal blockage points (numbered 1 through 6 in Figure 12) showed cause-and-effect relationships. These relationships seriously handicapped the plant's operations. A discussion of the significance of these blockage points follows.

1. Point one is the "product blockage," i.e., the product's long lead time in relation to the demands of the competitive market. Essentially, however, this lead time resulted from other blockage points, particularly the second.

2. Point two illustrates the most typical "horizontal blockages," i.e., structural compartmentalization. These blockages occurred at the divisions and boundaries separating various phases of the work process, such as market research, product design, product preparation, and production. They took the form of disagreements, misunderstandings, or feelings of superiority. They stifled internal motivation and created conflictual relationships.

3. Point three describes the "vertical blockages" par excellence, which occurred at the lower levels of the organization, in the teams. These arose primarily from the fragmentation of responsibility among four hierarchical levels of management and extreme job specialization. They led to an increased emphasis on ineffective remedial approaches and a stifling of creative individualism in the front lines of the organization.

4. Point four indicates junctures where numerous "unblocking meetings" were held. These meetings gradually produced the phenomenon of "sliding," in which the upper

management gravitated downward to resolve any problems that arose at the lower levels. The most direct result of this phenomenon was the creation of negative attitudes at the lower levels.

5. Point five depicts the role of labor representatives. The unions were highly integrated into the remedial process and played an important unblocking role. This was the specific source and foundation for their grievance-mongering attitude.

6. Finally, point six designates various personnel management and control methods. These methods sustained other blockages, created a grievance-mongering attitude, and reinforced external motivation.

These highly structured blockages raised unproductive costs, increased redundancy, divided and demotivated the employees, dispersed efforts, and generated negative attitudes. Such circumstances explain the plant's long lead time in relation to the demands of the competitive market.

Internal Motivation Creates Flexibility
(see Figure 4, quadrant 12)

Many companies were able to either prevent the creation of these typical blockages or remove them after the crisis came. The consistent characteristic of these blockages is their demotivating effect, for they prevent utilization of creative individualism and personal abilities. When equipment automation is impossible or requires major investment, creative individualism is the only factor that ensures financial success in a competitive market.

In the region where Raymond Dupont's plant was located, there was one small company whose operations were based on full use of personal potential and abilities. Its employees' internal motivation was unleashed by the elimination of hierarchical relationships and by considerable overlapping of various functions.

That company, which had fewer than 100 employees, broke with long-standing organizational principles because it had to adapt to a very competitive market. It in fact participated in a very delicate market. The customers had personal technical and design requirements, and they often imposed short delivery deadlines. Such orders upset the traditional production system and consequently were inappropriate for companies that wanted to maintain mass production.

This market niche was difficult but useful during a period of crisis. There was consequently no intensive specialization or hierarchical ordering of relationships in that small plant. It was not necessary to make jobs static and immobile, thereby creating conflicts of interest. On the contrary, it was necessary to unleash internal motivation.

The workers were versatile, but as in Dupont's team they had personal predilections in line with their technical interests and abilities. Consequently, the jobs were not classified. No one measured the contribution of each employee. This was an unusual but highly motivating situation because each person could prove his capability and competence.

In the early 1970s, the French government would certainly have required this employer to conform to the industry-wide collective agreement for metallurgy work. The law at that time mandated schedules that were included in the agreements adopted at the highest level, which were intended to cover any situation found throughout industry.

That small plant, however, was a specific result of the crisis. Since the work load decreased in the mass production sector, this employer, out of necessity, settled into an unusual market niche where there was still work. Requiring the employer to conform to a collective agreement under these circumstances would have meant immediate business failure. Nothing in the metallurgy agreement provided for the particular requirements of a special market.

In that special market, the schedule had to be completely flexible, and the work required extreme availability. The customers' special demands presupposed adaptations and ongoing technical innovations. However, there was no engineering department to formulate them, and establishing an engineering department would have been so expensive that the plant could not have sustained the cost.

In short, for financial reasons, it was impossible to apply the principle of specialization of functions in the organization of work. Employees were simultaneously workers (who performed machining and assembly work), set-up staff (who handled tooling problems), inspectors (who conducted quality control tests), and technicians (because they assumed responsibility for research and technical innovations).

The situation would have made life difficult for defenders of classification and detailed job descriptions. In fact, in this small plant, each person integrated several job categories, several functions, and several traditional hierarchical levels into his or her work. As a result, administrative and management authority and responsibilities were, to a large extent, regrouped at the worker level.

The same tendency existed in Dupont's team, but it was, of course, less well developed because of the hostility of the corporate work environment. However, despite such obstacles, his workers regained jobs that logically should have been the team's responsibility but that, because of the principle of specialization, were assigned either to administrative departments or to higher management levels.

Dupont was unable to go further in that direction. In contrast, the small employer in question pushed the system to the extreme, out of technical, financial, and commercial necessity.

Vertical and Horizontal Influence Increases Creativity
(see Figure 4, quadrants 11, 12)

Essentially, what were the employees in the small, specialized company? Were they workers, technicians, or supervisors? In fact, they participated in most phases and functions of the work process (horizontal or administrative specialization), but they also took part in its organization (the vertical or management function). The technical and commercial demands of this market niche eliminated the traditional specialization of the job categories and the hierarchical structure. They also sidestepped or discarded customary job classifications.

Orders were discussed among all those who would be involved in filling them. This contact with the marketing function was highly motivating and also pinpointed those special customer requirements and wishes that were likely to present new technical problems. In this manner, everyone was included in the technical and scheduling function.

The employer, who knew the employees well, sounded them out and asked them questions about new technical problems. They discussed problems together and formulated theories, and then each person thought them through before making a decision. They even thought about them at home. These were problems that concerned *them*. In the absence of various specialized functions that would have given them the "answer," they had to find it on their own. As a result, each person had a lasting horizontal and vertical influence, considerably exceeding the usual scope of a job position.

How can such a job be classified by traditional means? Did the rejection of extreme specialization constitute a "labor injustice"? Wasn't it, rather, an intelligent adaptation of the work organization to market constraints? Wasn't the employees' influence an efficiency factor that enabled the plant to operate and even to progress? And wasn't this same contribution also a means for these employees to apply their personal strengths? Finally, wasn't such a flexible and developmental organization also a factor in a good work atmosphere and combining individual efforts?

The employees of the specialized company did not ask themselves such questions because they were comfortable in their work. This was evident in the fact that, quite often, the answer to a difficult technical problem would spring to mind at home, during dinner or in front of the television. The employee who had the idea would visit his coworkers on the order. They would discuss it together. Then, they would all go to the plant, in the middle of the night. The employer would be alerted and come in to join them. They would conduct tests for several hours to check out the new idea.

In what classification system could such work be arranged, ranked, and described? Where would "availability" or "imagination" fit in? What about "coming up with an idea" or "testing in the middle of the night"? And what about "horizontal and vertical employee influence"?

In this small plant, where each person was familiar with the market situation and the file of outstanding orders, individual and group activity clearly could not be measured by the traditional means. But what about wages?

Because the employees knew each other quite well, and because each person's input was known by all, it was not hard to agree on wage levels. They compared these levels to the plant's financial prospects and its outstanding orders, rather than to the wage scales in a collective bargaining agreement.

It is true that the practices of this small plant, adhered to by all employees, encroach on the principle of "equal work, equal pay." It is quite possible that the "worker-technicians" would have been paid better for the same work by some large companies. But in these difficult times, jobs have become scarce, and most large companies have no worker-technician jobs.

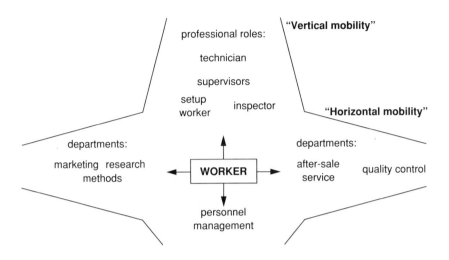

Figure 13.

Some workers left, for family or job security reasons or because the plant's market was difficult and fluctuating. But people left with regret in every instance. How do you calculate the importance of a job where there is interest in the work, a good atmosphere, overall responsibility, trust placed in each person, and horizontal and vertical influence?

These values, however, which play an important role in individual and group motivation, did indeed exist in that plant. They existed in Dupont's team as well, despite unfavorable conditions.

Success with Individualized Organizations
(see Figure 4, quadrants 11, 12)

The small plant held its own in a difficult market and achieved a certain amount of expansion because its operational structure was prepared to remove most of the costly blockages that burdened Dupont's plant. In fact, this type of developmental operational structure, which created motivating values and horizontal and vertical influence for everyone, promotes the use of employees' intelligence and skills and focusing of efforts.

A review of the most typical blockages (1 through 6 in Figure 12) observed in the operation of Dupont's plant presents an interesting picture, when viewed in the context of this small company.

"Product blockage," number 1 in the diagram, did not exist. Innovative marketing allowed the plant to settle into a niche that did not interest other companies in the same business sector. But it still had to adapt the organization of its work to the difficult and special constraints of that niche. That goal was achieved through organizational innovations, making it possible to bring the jobs out of their traditionally narrow confines. In this way, horizontal and vertical influence was gradually created in jobs.

Blockage 2, which took the form of conflicts on the administrative level between various phases of the work process, was prevented. First, the process was significantly streamlined. Then, through horizontal influence, workers participated in every phase, from taking orders to delivering finished products and after-sale service. This multiphase participation cultivated a passion for technical innovation, and most of the risks, downtime, and unnecessary inventory and handling were eliminated.

Blockage 3, which occurs in the lower levels of the organization by bringing teams in conflict with the upper management as well as certain operational departments, was also prevented in that company. This was because the workers handled most of the responsibilities (inspection, setting up, work organization, research) that, in a rigid organization, justified the existence of middle-management levels and specialized departments.

At the same time, this regrouping of authority and responsibilities averted the use of the most common remedial means. It streamlined the work and reduced unproductive costs to a minimum. And since, in addition, this regrouping was motivating, the work atmosphere was good and tasks could be assigned according to personal strengths and abilities. In sum, this approach ensured a strong personal contribution by each employee. For that reason, the employees could be evaluated on the basis of their contribution and outputs and not on the traditional classification of jobs.

Consequently, blockage 4, the "sliding" downward of the management hierarchy, was not present. The workers' vertical influence made it unnecessary to create the middle-management levels that are so numerous in large companies. Dupont's plant had three levels; by their very existence, they made it impossible to motivate teams, except in the isolated enclaves.

Blockage 5, which is related to the remedial role of the unions, was also avoided. Since there was no intermediary from the corporate hierarchy, there was no need for a labor organization intermediary. Individual problems were handled directly by the interested parties, usually with the participation of those who worked with them.

And finally, the sixth traditional blockage, produced by rigid, standardized personnel management methods, no longer existed either. This was because the employees were evaluated collectively, and each one managed the use of his or her time according to the requirements of the work. Promotions did not entail the creation of hierarchical jobs, which in a rigid organization served as symbolic rewards. In this small company, promotion meant broader or greater responsibility, enhanced collective recognition, and, to the extent possible, better wages.

It is indeed possible to unleash internal motivation and draw on employees' creative potential. As the examples of the small specialized company and Raymond Dupont's team illustrate, it can be done by calling on the skill of innovators. Innovators can be found on any team or in any department. They are people who do not hesitate to replace the rigid organizational principles with other organizational principles that are better suited to the profound ongoing change. They unblock jobs and eliminate the outmoded constraints that narrowly limit the tapping of knowledge and creative individualism. Innovators must be "discovered" — and they must be allowed to act.

In the case of Dupont's team, the elimination of the individual output system broadened the employees' field of activity in accordance with their own internal motivation. The number, repetition, and rate of production steps to be performed ceased to be narrow limitations. Dupont even introduced his workers to areas reserved for managers and administrators. Modifying equipment, implementing small innovations, tooling and small maintenance jobs were all functions of operational departments and the management hierarchy.

The small specialized company went much further than the machine shop foreman was able to go. Its rigid organization disappeared, and most of the responsibilities were integrated into the jobs on the front lines of the organization.

This kind of change and adaptation to the competitive conditions were possible in the foreman's plant as well, despite its large size. The utilization of such an opening depended on management's awareness and strategy. Such openings were blocked, however, by resistance to change. The intensity of this resistance generally is directly proportional to the degree of complexity of the organizational structure and to the level of rigid specialization of administrative authority and responsibilities.

This is readily understandable in that each organizational system spontaneously selects employees at all levels in accordance with its own criteria. A rigid organization, which had to ensure stable, constant production for an unsaturated market, required good performers in the lower ranks of the organization and also good specialists in the upper management levels who could resolve unforeseen situations and special problems.

In contrast, an individualized organization, which responds to competitive market imperatives, needs other qualities and personal abilities. It requires employees who dare to take initiative on the front lines of the organization, good facilitators to create bonds between the teams and the management, and good coordinators to head units, effectively unifying and combining efforts.

There is a huge difference between these two choices. However, when the criterion of specialization must be replaced by the individualization demanded by the changing market, the selection criteria must also be changed. It is precisely this change that inevitably causes resistance at all levels. Decision makers selected according to the criteria of a rigid organization are not always able to adapt to new efficiency criteria.

Raymond Dupont's boss, the production manager, was a good specialist, but could not adapt. His personal inclination and training prevented him from becoming a good coordinator. In the new competitive situation, his personal qualities no longer met the requirements of his job. Nor did the production unit manager and the head foremen support Dupont's experiment after it was discovered. In fact, the idea of transferring management authority and responsibility to the worker level was contrary to their own ambition and to the actual rationale for their jobs.

The same was true for certain operational departments, which were very attached to the feeling of superiority that their role provided them. They too were hostile to the idea of overlapping functions.

In a small company, where rigid organization is not applied with customary rigor, resistance to change is generally weak. Even in Dupont's plant, however, it was possible to overcome resistance. Reducing the corporate hierarchy to three basic functions (facilitators, coordinators, and top management) — an idea accepted by the corporate management — thus permitted the development of a spirit of initiative in the teams and at the facilitators' level. The rest depended mainly on the strategy and approach used during corrective action. A gradual approach and the use of "anchoring points" can overcome resistance to change by expanding an experiment team by team, unit by unit, building each time on the knowledge acquired. This was possible because the anchoring points were already detached from the old rigid organization and, at the same time, they were not engaged in a remedial approach. Instead, they had a new operational structure, i.e., an individualized organization.

To tap this potential to the fullest, however, complementary relationships first had to be created between the three basic functions. The dispersed responsibilities had to be regrouped to unleash internal motivation. That goal was difficult to achieve. From such a perspective, the traditional, ponderous, and hierarchically structured organization chart had to give way to a set of three complementary and considerably overlapping functions (see Figure 14). From this perspective, decision makers in those three basic functions are distinguished not so much by their place in the corporate hierarchy as by their complementary tasks.

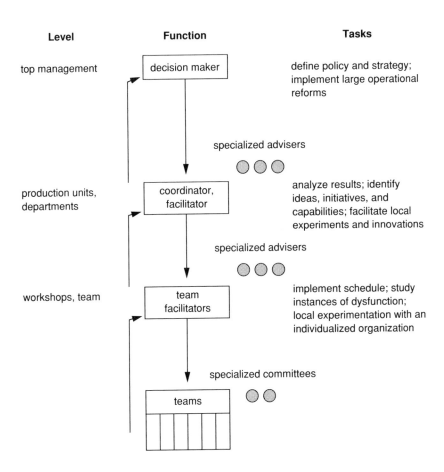

Level	Function	Tasks
top management	decision maker	define policy and strategy; implement large operational reforms
	specialized advisers	
production units, departments	coordinator, facilitator	analyze results; identify ideas, initiatives, and capabilities; facilitate local experiments and innovations
	specialized advisers	
workshops, team	team facilitators	implement schedule; study instances of dysfunction; local experimentation with an individualized organization
	specialized committees	
	teams	

Figure 14.

CHAPTER NINE

Spreading Successful Results

Reforms Precede Application of a Successful Experiment
(see Figure 3, quadrant 22; Figure 4, quadrant 11)

In a small or medium-sized company, it is possible to set up an individualized organization quite rapidly. That task, on the other hand, seems to be much more difficult to carry out in large companies, particularly those in countries that are still immersed in the tradition of rigid organization, extremely hierarchical structuring, and strictly regulated operations. An operational structure based on intensive specialization of jobs, hierarchical ordering of relationships, and the regulatory role of government intensely resists change.

Why is this so? The answer lies in the fact that this structure is a source of prestige and power. As a result, it often stifles true internal motivation, replacing it with hierarchical ambition, which creates divisions among employees and fragments their efforts.

For this reason, a highly competitive economy requires a flexible operational structure without blockages so that work can be individualized. Stifled internal motivation can reemerge, if working conditions change and become stimulating.

The revival of stifled or distorted motivation was possible in Raymond Dupont's plant. Organizational and structural reforms were needed, of course, to reinforce the successful experiments. These experiments formed the "anchoring points" for reforms.

Anchoring points existed throughout the plant, but they were widely dispersed. Coordinator positions were held by front-line foremen and by unit managers. It would be necessary to initiate some changes in order for a unit manager to be assisted by innovators from the lower ranks, and for the innovators to have a coordinator above them on whom they could rely as they took action.

Hence, openings did exist. The situation was not completely blocked. An "anchoring point" like Dupont's skill group made it possible to adapt the unit's organization to new technical and commercial constraints. The specific tasks necessary for proper fulfillment of the three functions could be entrusted to specialized advisers who were not hierarchical intermediaries.

There were three advantages to this approach:

- Responsibilities were *regrouped* in one unit instead of being fragmented among six levels of management and several operational departments.
- Relationships between the three jobs became *complementary* so as to facilitate the study and resolution of operational problems.
- The regrouping of responsibilities and the creation of complementary relationships *unleashed internal motivation*, which had been stifled by fragmented roles and subordinate relationships.

The regrouping of authority, duties, and responsibilities once fragmented among the various levels of management and many departments has one practical advantage in particular. If an urgent or serious problem arises, it becomes possible to react much more quickly than in a situation where the same responsibilities are fragmented horizontally and vertically.

Anchoring Points Anticipate Change
(see Figure 4, quadrants 11, 12)

It is possible to create a motivating operational structure based on individualized organization, even in a large company, by starting with a few anchoring points.

In fact, if decision makers and coordinators develop those anchoring points, if they recognize and acknowledge their achievements and innovations, and finally, if they support their development, such anchoring points will quickly become true learning centers for the departments and other teams.

Such centers can exert a strong influence on their environment. Their results incite curiosity. Their attractive work environment generates a desire to follow their example. The recognition of their ability to innovate creates new evaluation criteria.

Thus, it is possible to gradually build at a few anchoring points an operational structure that will develop creative individualism among employees. Such a course of action must, of course, be long term because it is necessary to revise the procedures of the rigid, "remedial" organization one by one, and replace them with other, more effective procedures. It will be particularly difficult in the beginning to gradually modify habits, attitudes, and evaluation criteria — in other words, to change individual and group behavior. That behavior is both sustained by, and provides support for, the operational structure in effect.

Dupont's approach was exemplary in that regard. He was a good strategist. He moved forward simultaneously on both planes (team organization and employee behavior), seizing specific opportunities to go a little further. Generally speaking, he modified old habits prior to creating new procedures, such as working in tandem on flexible jobs. By responding to his work-ers' "need for independence" and gradually expanding the excessively narrow limitations of their jobs, he paved the way for a change in organizational structure. That change, in turn, unleashed internal motivation.

Such a complex but effective approach explains why it is important to first identify existing anchoring points before embarking on an ambitious reform project. In fact, when under-taking such a course of action, it is not possible to get results with a deductive, administrative approach that mandates change from higher up. In such instances, managerial directives are not only ineffectual or fleetingly effective but also dangerous because failure can have a discouraging effect. Furthermore, if employees are not prepared beforehand, directives are likely to create an attitude of resistance. In that case, a reform project can turn into a costly conflict. Since the onset of the economic crisis, this has been a typical phenomenon.

When a decision maker or a facilitator becomes aware of the need to develop an individualized organization (the only type of organization that can respond effectively and without addi-tional cost to a significant increase in customers' special demands), the first task is to identify anchoring points. This is a way to ensure an important alliance and, at the same time, adopt an approach that will secure compliance by teams and production units, rather than arousing their distrust.

Identifying future centers of attraction is at once a *strategic* task (seeking an alliance) and a *methodological* task (choosing a suitable approach).

Such anchoring points are sometimes quite well known. Efficient teams and departments coexist with less efficient ones that are oriented toward tinkering and costly "clever tactics." In such cases, small enclaves can quite easily become the pre-ferred work style. This depends, above all, on the role of the coordinators.

In other situations where tradition is still very strong (as in Raymond Dupont's plant), anchoring points are usually ignored because the criteria for efficiency and evaluation are either antiquated or directed at remedial action rather than enlistment of personal potential and abilities.

Particularly in such situations, identification requires detailed studies. The results of these studies generally astonish senior managers because they were unaware that there were strong and effective employees throughout the plant. Such prior study is strategic in nature because it determines the basis for future action. It is therefore the first major step in reforming a shop or production unit.

Several kinds of indicators were used for such studies. The first group consists of well-known *financial indicators* such as output, quality control results, unproductive costs, and absenteeism rates. Technical and financial coefficients are applied to a limited degree throughout. Therefore, the results sometimes reveal a considerable variation from one team or production unit to another.

The reasons for such differences are rarely clear. Raymond Dupont's team was never criticized because it had good results. Upper management, however, was content to explain them away as luck or the "good attitude" of the team members, rather than asking themselves how such an attitude was created, since it did not exist elsewhere.

But asking such questions would have amounted to deviating from a remedial approach. This is why, at that plant, it was difficult to take the first step. In fact, management's thinking was oriented toward stereotyped responses, which obviously were a substitute for strategic studies.

For that reason, in many instances, managers simply record good results, without using them with an eye toward rectifying problems. Those who go no further in their understanding obviously do not use the other coefficients, which are more significant than the first ones.

The second group of indicators refers to the *collective environment and the different motivations* in a team, in relation to the organizational system. The effects of an operational structure on individual and collective attitudes can be implicitly recognized.

This type of study links financial context to the interpersonal and personal context. It is not well suited to highly specialized managers, who often have no technical training but who must find the causes of inefficiency in areas other than their specialty, particularly with respect to various organizational factors.

Such a handicap becomes even more significant when applying the third group of indicators, which actually entails the study of *employees' personal qualities and abilities*. The study culminates in individualizing efficiency factors, since, in actuality, they are individual in nature.

The various levels of the management hierarchy in any sector usually give a fairly wide variety of responses to one-time problems and problems with operational procedures, with some rather general tendencies. Thus, certain responses are emotional reactions rather than logical perceptions. The danger in this situation is that emotion rarely succeeds in distinguishing one-time problems from problems with the operational structure. Emotion is a feeling generated by a phenomenon or an event, not by the study of such phenomena or events.

But even a logical understanding often prevents deeper analysis of problems encountered, especially when "remedial responses" are deeply entrenched in people's minds. In such cases, there will be no action or experimentation.

Raymond Dupont had his own direct knowledge and experience of these various tendencies. At first, seized by fear of the unknown, he reacted emotionally to the team's problems. However, he succeeded in rapidly changing his approach, while his colleagues moved toward remedial methods. In this way, he differentiated himself from them more and more, as he endeavored to implement an individualized organization.

These different tendencies are illustrated in Figure 15. The anchoring points are found in zone 14. When a coordinator succeeds in identifying and locating them and understanding their causes and effects, he can then embark on an ambitious reform strategy. Anchoring points usually bring valid responses to the sector's technical and commercial constraints.

Such responses are not, however, easily accepted by those who find themselves in the impasse zones. Those who are well

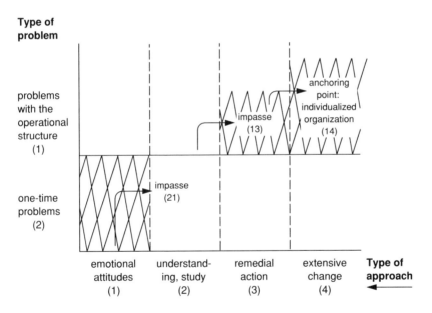

- The impasse (quadrant 21) is the result of emotional approaches (fearful attitude, the pursuit of security). In this case, even one-time problems become intrusive.

- The impasse (quadrant 13) is the result of remedial actions. In this case, one-time problems are resolved (but at the price of sometimes enormous non-value-adding costs), but problems with the operational structure remain.

- The anchoring point (quadrant 14): even certain problems with the operational structure receive inadequate responses.

Figure 15.

settled in their remedial roles do not see the need to change their approach because they *do* solve one-time problems. Those who are always overwhelmed or have a highly emotional attitude are afraid of any change. They will even risk becoming aggressive if they are forced to alter their working methods.

Raymond Dupont might have been able to influence his colleagues who belonged in these various categories. But in the old structure, in which he was subordinated to three higher levels of management, this was not possible.

A Strategy for Freeing Anchoring Points
from Corporate Meddling
(see Figure 4, quadrants 12, 22)

Transforming an anchoring point into a "center of attraction" requires facilitating its influence on others. Coordinators are crucial to this process, since their role is to free the anchoring point from meddling by the corporate hierarchy.

From this perspective, a coordinator is successful at this task to the extent that he or she becomes a facilitator. In fact, exerting a constructive influence over the different teams requires building contacts among them. There were no such contacts in the Dupont's machining unit. There were none between the teams or the foremen.

There was absolutely no need for such contacts because their role was handled by intermediaries from the corporate hierarchy. For that reason, the foreman did not form skill groups in which complementary roles and mutual assistance between workers could develop. The workers certainly knew one another, but the traditional organizational structure created barriers between them.

Consequently, in such an instance, a facilitator would have to create suitable conditions to ensure that the lessons from an effective experiment were conveyed. Creating such conditions requires some time, and the process must be gradual. Such is the case with technical issues, as well.

Replacing an old product or releasing a new model on the market requires long-term research and testing, with no short-cuts. The same is true for problems with operational procedures. The facilitator should therefore increase the number of meetings with interested parties to publicize the results of the experimental group, describing and clarifying the foremen's various approaches and comparing their advantages and disadvantages.

Only after this preparatory stage should the facilitator undertake a course of action that would replace the conventional organization chart with a structure that facilitates contact and the transfer of authority and responsibility.

In this respect as well, Raymond Dupont's experimental approach can be considered an example to follow. The front-line supervisors could combine themselves into a skill group. In this way, the machine shop, instead of existing as rigorously separated teams, could be managed by that group of supervisors.

Such a change would be significant in relation to the traditional rigid organization chart (Figure 16). This type of organizational structure is still used quite often in the manufacturing and service industries. It was obviously designed for stable production circumstances in which services and products of all kinds had a long life cycle, one-time problems were few and routine, machining jobs were highly specialized, and negative individualism was so highly developed that it was necessary to isolate the employees in teams.

But this rigorous and highly regimented structure no longer suited the new economic situation, in which the number of different disturbances was on the rise, both in terms of one-time problems and problems with the operational structure. Rather than isolating and separating the employees in teams, it was necessary to bring them together by implementing a supervisor skill group (Figure 17).

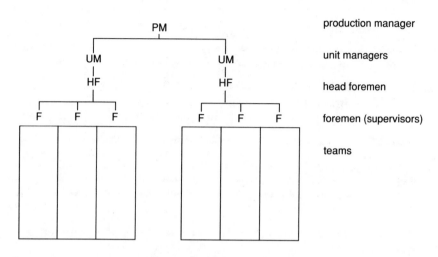

production manager

unit managers

head foremen

foremen (supervisors)

teams

Figure 16. A Traditional Organizational Chart

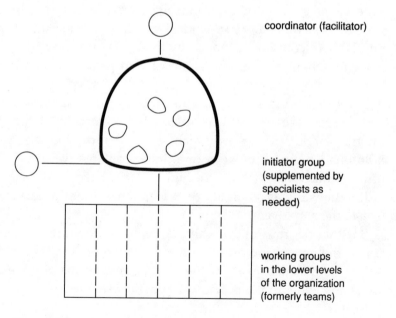

coordinator (facilitator)

initiator group
(supplemented by
specialists as
needed)

working groups
in the lower levels
of the organization
(formerly teams)

Figure 17. The New Structure for Flexibility

Compared to the conventional organization chart, the new structure shows distinct features because it replaces subordinate relationships with complementary relationships, thus facilitating the use of personal potential and abilities.

The first striking feature of this structural model is the great simplification of the production management structure, which is reduced from four levels to two.

Next, isolation in teams gives way to a skill group of supervisors placed at the head of the work unit. The group can be reinforced if necessary by one or two advisers who specialize in technical or management issues.

This structure has already proved effective in many instances, even though its new look runs counter to traditional thinking. Such a structure is, however, much more suitable than the old organization chart in situations in which a company's market environment increasingly mandates "customized modifications" of the product. In such instances, the number of special and unique problems increases dramatically. If problems with the operational structure slow the resolution of such problems, bottlenecks are created in the operating levels of the organization. This causes a climate of constant irritation and the development of negative individualism.

Dupont's team illustrated the problem and also resolved it. Such a situation, in which employees feel continually stretched beyond their former limitations, presupposes great flexibility, which neither the old rigid organization nor the remedial system can provide. By creating a supervisors' skill group at the head of the work unit, the foreman was able to influence his colleagues and attract them gradually toward the development of an individualized organization.

But there are other advantages in the new structure as well. Within the context of the old organization chart, foremen did in fact have to face a wide variety of problems, even when they were not well trained in those particular areas. That deficiency was used to justify the creation of middle-management levels to assume responsibility for resolving such problems.

However, that approach, applied uniformly, overlooked the personal abilities and knowledge of the foremen. While it did fill certain voids, it was, on the other hand, frustrating for those who felt deprived of responsibilities that they could have handled. However, no exceptions could be made because the intermediaries (head foremen, unit managers) outranked the foremen in the organizational hierarchy. Consequently, subordinate relationships, rather than complementary roles, were created.

All of these drawbacks, which stand in the way of proper application of the knowledge and abilities of the team's supervisors, disappear within a skill group. The first reason for this is that the participants do not have hierarchical relationships. Instead, they rapidly develop reciprocal and cooperative relationships.

Second — and this was the most important feature of Raymond Dupont's experiment — in a skill group, the participants can find their own direction based on their inclination, training, and abilities. They can seek out areas that particularly interest them and in which they feel internally motivated.

Dupont, for example, proved himself to be very competent in the organization of work and in the experimental approach. Some of his colleagues, who had a flair for direct personal contact, were especially able to handle liaison with the departments. Others, who were particularly interested in product quality, were able to develop joint efforts with quality control, and so forth.

In each of these instances, the workers had attentive, well-placed spokespersons. In addition, by pointing out the effects of dysfunctions within the unit, Dupont influenced the coordinator position (i.e., the production manager), so that the latter would assume responsibility for problems related to the system of individual output, classification, and wages.

In short, through a profound structural change, the flexibility already developed in Dupont's team was able to penetrate other teams and rapidly become more universally introduced.

Tactics for Using the Anchoring Points
(see Figure 4, quadrant 12, 22)

This approach, which consists of various stages or phases, can be used in all types of companies in the manufacturing and service sectors. Assertive managers and anchoring points exist everywhere.

The advantage of such an approach is that it is flexible and gradual. It makes it possible to rely initially on one team that is more advanced than the others, in attempting to develop any entire area. Like a puzzle, the first anchoring point is developed and expanded, exerting influence over an ever-widening environment.

However, for such a course of action to succeed, the approach must also be experimental, making sure workers grasp the need to change. It is this aspect that ensures a sequencing of stages:

1. Identifying new anchoring points
2. Analyzing the "actors" (alliances that make it possible to develop a strategy)
3. Paving the way (applying new evaluation criteria, comparing approaches used by the departmental and production unit managers)
4. Facilitating the establishment of a skill group
5. Institutionalizing structural change
6. Stabilizing the results achieved.

The application of these different stages, as well as their sequence and duration, depend on the environment one wishes to develop. In Dupont's machining area, for example, the first stage was important; in many other instances, one could pass directly over it to later stages.

Under favorable conditions, "paving the way" might not be needed, but in Dupont's shop it had to be done with great care. In his case, an outside consultant had to analyze the actors, since the production manager was not prepared to perform that task. In such cases, the decision maker played an especially important role in unblocking the situation; he had to choose whether to gamble on the personal development of the unit manager or to replace him.

In the machine shop, the unit manager's job was given to another manager, who was less proficient in mechanics than his predecessor but was capable of recognizing the effects of problems with the operational structure and discussing them with employees.

This unblocking action made it possible to recognize and acknowledge the efficiency of Dupont's team and have its progress discussed at meetings.

The three foremen in the first production unit quickly formed a skill group. Then, several months later, the foremen in the second production unit, with one exception, followed suit. Some time later, the two production units combined, so five foremen belonged to the skill group. The sixth preferred to remain in a special advisory position. The old middle managers opted for change. But rapid development of creative individualism was still not ensured.

When conclusive results of an experiment begin emerging in other teams and then reach the entire production unit, it is possible, after consolidating the new structure, to think about expanding, protracting, and establishing it in other production areas and in operational departments.

The machine shop's direct downstream associates were the assembly shop (for which the parts were machined), the quality control department, and the maintenance department. Upstream, they were the purchasing and production scheduling departments. The machine shop was directly interested in their results, since some of these associates in particular determined its own efficiency, to a large degree.

By starting with a single team and then going beyond the confines of the production unit, the individualized organization could therefore win over the area surrounding the pilot area to develop creative individualism there as well.

This expansion of the experiment displays to advantage the good performance attained and resists most stereotyped explanations. In addition, it can encourage all those in other work areas who suffer from incessant and repetitious problems and who, when they see an achievement, hope to be able to duplicate it. On the strategic level, it is a true search for alliances.

The machine shop needed such an expansion to change traditional rigid relationships with its associates. Under new economic circumstances, the various phases of the work process had to overlap rather than be compartmentalized. Part Four discusses this overlapping in more detail.

PART FOUR

Transferring Operations and Labor Relations to the Front Lines

Raymond Dupont's experiment, which added flexibility to jobs, went well beyond the first stage of employee motivation. By penetrating the domain formerly occupied by management, operational departments, and social functions, it also demonstrated the existence of developmental potential that was as yet unexplored. The assumption of certain operational and labor relations responsibilities could develop even more creative individualism in teams and could redirect various departments toward important work demanded by escalating competition.

In this evolutionary perspective, corporate management committed to reducing the organization chart to three basic functions and placing certain previously hierarchical roles in a horizontal or advisory position. These roles proved useful.

After structural reform, which facilitated the transfer of new authority and responsibilities to supervisors and teams, the experiment was extended throughout the machine shop. It was a decisive step toward applying creative individualism. Next, before taking a second step forward, it was necessary to reinforce the knowledge acquired by formulating the organizational procedures and relationships that would replace the demotivating mechanisms of rigid operational structure.

Formulating procedures and relationships is truly laborious work. It usually holds little interest for theoreticians, who are content with tracing the developmental profiles of organizations. Nevertheless, it directly influences the motivation for work. In fact, if new operational mechanisms are not put into place, the old mechanisms may return at any time and block development. This explains the methodological importance of such know-how, particularly during a period of change.

In the machining area, the new basic mechanisms onto which the others were subsequently grafted included *collective output* and the practice of *distributing tasks according to personal aptitudes*. These mechanisms are closely interrelated.

Collective output was quickly expanded by other mechanisms, such as rotation, mobility, and versatility. The new task distribution created supplementary jobs and small improvements. These two types of mechanisms, however, required many exchanges, quick meetings on scheduling or results, and longer meetings to discuss output and improvements. Such exchanges and meetings likewise became operational mechanisms for the teams and for the supervisor groups.

These mechanisms were supported by a variety of relationships, such as tandems, subgroups based on affinity and complementarity, and personal and group affinities that had been stifled in the individual output system.

The various organizational mechanisms and relationships made it possible to evaluate personal contributions much more precisely than under the old classification system. Evaluation was quickly transformed into a group procedure that took place at monthly meetings.

Ultimately, through that intensive collective experience, new values and considerations emerged within the teams. They formalized evaluation criteria and made it possible to measure the significance of different personal contributions to the collective output. The most highly regarded criterion was innovation, followed by availability to listen or assist, and precision. An actual scale of criteria was drafted with the consent of team members.

New operational mechanisms and evaluation criteria replaced the old constraints and classification system. They compelled the teams to penetrate the area of authority and responsibility for operations and labor relations.

After the expansion of Raymond Dupont's experiment, the supervisor group and the other teams also formulated different operational mechanisms to replace the old hierarchical relationships and organizational constraints. They also quickly eliminated the petty conflicts that previously had erupted in the machine shops.

The individual output system and the corresponding classification system had generated many different conflicts. In fact, it was unusual to see an exact match between the objectively defined content of a job and the personal qualities of the jobholder. This was true not only because of the wide variety of personal abilities, but also because even those employees who did not possess the required abilities tried hard to get high-ranking jobs, which paid more. This was an ambiguous and even antagonistic kind of motivation. The desire to earn more was inconsistent with the abilities and preferences not required by the job. The phenomenon was similar to the idea of replacing internal motivation with hierarchical ambition, which was often the only way to get a promotion.

The general outcome of these antagonistic motivations was a feeling of dissatisfaction and sometimes even frustration. It was one of the most frequent sources of petty conflicts, even in the upper levels of management. On the front lines of the organization, such conflicts constantly threatened to turn into labor disputes, since it was not possible to resolve personal problems within an impersonal specialization system. It was therefore necessary to modify the system of classification, i.e., the value and hierarchical ordering of the jobs. Such modifications systematically became the fulcrum in the balance of power between labor and management. Gradually the classification system lost much of its supposed "objective nature" and reflected instead the balance of power in the plant.

Through reforms, new organizational mechanisms and relationships eliminated the root causes of petty conflicts. The number of such conflicts dropped significantly.

The rapid evolution of new operational mechanisms ultimately brought up the question of authority and responsibility for operations and labor relations (personnel management), which had always been grouped in the departments and the employee relations office.

Once again, management made a dual decision to overlap certain mechanisms, powers, and responsibilities and gradually transfer other authority and responsibility to the teams and supervisor groups.

Implementing this new stage was a delicate operation. It had to be carried out prudently, gradually, and skillfully. Learning new operational mechanisms also developed financial judgment within the teams, gradually linking employees with the company's bottom-line progress. From then on, technical, financial, and market data were no longer abstract figures. They were evidence of intensive participation by teams and the work areas in the company's operations.

The unions experienced this evolution with a certain amount of distress — at first because they lost their customary high-ranking spokespersons, and subsequently because petty conflicts were being resolved within the teams instead of turning into labor disputes. Consequently, union representatives could not avoid the evolution of their own roles.

CHAPTER TEN

The Organizational Mechanisms

The Old Demotivating Mechanisms
(see Figure 4, quadrant 22)

The machine shop's transformation was launched from one anchoring point, i.e., the foreman's team. In practice, however, continuing the strategic course of action was complex and difficult.

In fact, the old operational structure in that work area was based entirely on the principle of specialization of operator jobs, a legacy of the period of high economic growth. Nearly everything in that operational structure was ensured by means of external motivation, orders, instructions, and hierarchical relationships:

- The various levels of management had specialized remedial roles.
- The lowest levels of management, which perceived deficiencies and disturbances, had no overall responsibility.
- Information reached the upper levels of management but not those who needed it.
- Communication was unidirectional, with instructions moving from the top downward.

- Financial outcomes were criticized rather than analyzed.
- In the teams, the individual piecework system was reinforced by a multitude of different constraints.

Hence, the means of exerting pressure were omnipresent, and employees expended a large part of their energy and intelligence in combating and thwarting them. These means, however, were deeply rooted in tradition. As a result, they were reinforced by habit, old judgment criteria, hierarchical ambition, and, quite often, genuine conviction. High-level managers asserted that eliminating subordinate relationships would cause chaos and bungling.

Ultimately, this situation was similar to that of the French government, where the old roles lost the rationale for their existence in an economy where constraints change constantly and require speedy reactions on the part of commercial enterprises. Dismantling the old mechanisms for stability and uniform economic growth one by one and replacing them with other more suitable ones is not an easy course of action, either in a manufacturing plant or in government. Such mechanisms are at once structural, organizational, and behavioral in nature.

For this reason, even in a relatively modest work area like Raymond Dupont's machine shop, replacing the old mechanisms was not an easy task. In each instance, it was necessary to test in actual practice new mechanisms that relied on each employee's internal motivation and promoted the use of their personal abilities.

These experiments progressed rapidly in some instances and slowly in others. There was a wide range of situations, depending on the extent to which employees were conditioned. One person might find his "true motivation," stifled for many years, as soon as a constraint was removed. In another instance, supervisors would have to remain patient and use methods that also deconditioned and taught the person. Using new mechanisms did not always come naturally. In many cases they had to be learned.

In addition, this task of dismantling and replacing old mechanisms had to be carried out vertically as well as horizontally. To overcome the demotivating mechanisms connected with fragmented responsibilities, it was necessary to simplify the organizational structure and regroup fragmented roles. In order to eliminate the compartmentalization of the departments — and the resulting strained relations with production units — their respective functions had to be patiently overlapped.

And, in each instance, it was necessary to provide a training period for the interested parties. Without prior training, the regrouping of responsibilities can generate fear rather than motivation. Nor is horizontal decompartmentalization an obvious procedure, for the mechanisms of complementarity, reciprocity, and cooperation must be learned in practice.

For this reason, the expanded application of Raymond Dupont's experiment as a strategic course of action took two years, a reasonable amount of time for such an activity.

Analyzing the Players to Find Alliances
(see Figure 4, quadrant 11)

Reality is always more complex than theoretical schemes or operational models conceived on the basis of various hypotheses. This is because individuals and working groups vary widely in their reactions to the same system of regulations, organizational factors, or personnel management methods. Theoretical models and schemes can only partially account for these various attitudes and emotions, which complicate any program intended to change a working environment.

Such was the case with Raymond Dupont's team, which had a modest number of workers. That complexity could grow only if one envisioned expanding the experiment to the other five teams, the management structure, and even the different departments (environment) in the machine shop.

Nevertheless, the reason that the program succeeded in overcoming the growing number of obstacles was that, among the members of the supervisor's skill group, Dupont represented solid support and a wealth of experience.

Another reason was that the new production manager, who held the coordinator position, cooperated very well with the group, and especially with Dupont. In fact, at first, everything was based on that tandem. Success was therefore ensured by the appropriate strategic approach used by the two men. Through their collaboration, the many persistent obstacles were finally overcome:

- Rigid customs
- Negative attitudes
- Hierarchical reasoning
- Compartmentalized functions
- Rigid organizational factors and personnel management methods.

However, the degree of persistence of these obstacles *varied* from one individual to another, from team to team, and from department to department. This situation made it possible to use a strategic approach, and, in fact, to overcome the obstacles, a strategy was needed.

Dupont knew this quite well since, before establishing even one tandem in his team, he had to observe his workers and find the affinities and friendships that he could use as supports on the job. He built the tandems and small groups on those supports.

But when it came to adapting his team's individualized organization to a production unit, the dimension of the field of activity changed considerably. Consequently, Dupont had to think not only on an individual level but also on the level of the other five teams.

To influence them, he first had to explore the territory. He shared that task with his workers, who already had experience doing so. They provided him with the necessary information:

- Which people in the neighboring teams were attracted by the skill group's results?
- Which people were opposed to such a change?
- Why?
- What were the rumors about such a goal?
- Where did the union representatives stand on the changes?

Dupont also observed the reactions of his colleagues. One of them was curious to learn about his group. Another was afraid of the experiment. The third supervisor thought only about his own security. The fourth was waiting for some "proof." And the fifth was firmly rooted in the remedial resolution of problems.

Thus, Dupont spontaneously conducted an analysis of the actors and drew conclusions from it. He concerned himself only with his curious colleague because he could connect with him the most quickly. For him, that colleague represented an anchoring point.

Dupont's task during this phase was made difficult, however, by the presence of the head foremen and the production unit managers, who sensed danger. They knew that the new individualized organization meant that the middle levels of management were going to disappear. Since they were unable to imagine their future role as advisers or part of the supervisory group, they opposed pursuing that course of action. They did so principally by trying to demonstrate that the transformation disrupted work and brought nothing to the production units. But for the direct support of the new production manager, they would have blocked any change permanently.

This complex situation, in which the workers were observed for many months, was not easy to endure. Ultimately, the head foremen and the unit managers who earlier could not imagine being at the same level as their former subordinates, requested the change. Four foremen joined the group. The fifth (the one who favored "remedies") preferred to remain as an adviser.

The Supervisor Skill Group Learns How to Work

However, a total victory had not yet been won. It took many months for the group to take shape. The burden of long-standing habits was overwhelming. Habits tended to affect judgment, generate stereotypical responses to new problems, stifle strategic analyses, or cause highly emotional reactions.

Eliminating such automatic behavior was not an easy thing to do. One of the foremen, for example, wanted to assume responsibility for assigning the workers every morning to replace absentees when their jobs involved urgent work. He did this task by habit, however — authoritatively, without consulting his colleagues in the skill group. His manner of filling the gaps caused havoc, and in the end he had to be relieved of that responsibility.

From that time on, every morning, the whole supervisor group reviewed which positions needed to be filled. After analyzing the various situations, one of the group members would visit the teams involved. He would present the problem to the workers, they would discuss the schedule of priorities, and in this way, volunteers would be found to work with the short-handed team.

Training and breaking in the group of former foremen took a long time — nearly a year — because the rules of individual leadership were ingrained deeply in them. These rules had never espoused a sense of solidarity or mutual assistance.

The group finally came together because Dupont and the curious foreman formed a *tandem*. They shared their observations and had discussions before proceeding to resolve problems. When they went back to the office, they informed their coworkers. This nucleus ultimately influenced the other members of the group to abandon old negative attitudes.

It was necessary to constantly pick out and isolate old attitudes and old methods of work, demonstrate new mechanisms, compare results and run tests, and provide a training period for interested parties.

Through this course of action, the supervisor group progressed rapidly. But the group's environment — i.e., the different departments — continued to operate within their old habits. That contradiction ultimately became blatant and accelerated the course of events.

In the past, the various functional departments would always discuss schedule or priority changes, supply and maintenance problems, and quality control results for finished products with the machine shop's upper-level managers. But now there were no such managers, as the two middle levels had been abolished. Therefore, by organizational reflex, the departments wanted to handle the problems with the production manager alone. They were not looking for the most competent colleague; instead they sought the colleague highest on the organization chart.

To counter such a demotivating approach, the production manager at first had to handle questions directly with them. But soon he started to associate particular members of the supervisor group with these analyses, and these people showed themselves to be the most competent in the area concerned.

Then, instead of responding personally to questions posed by a department manager, the production manager began to direct questions to one of the supervisors to find out what he thought. More often than not, he accepted that response as his own. His way of doing things made it possible to shake loose the old firm convictions, make effective presentations, and create true professional relationships.

In this way, the production manager patiently accustomed his associates to the presence of the group members. In this instance, as always, the diversity of personalities played a positive role. In a few months, certain department managers finally changed their minds, shook off their characteristic hierarchical values, and accepted the idea that the members of the supervisor group could become legitimate spokespersons.

Decompartmentalizing Horizontal Relationships
(see Figure 4, quadrant 13)

After the two middle-management levels were abolished, making it possible to transfer certain management (vertical) authority and responsibility to the supervisor group, the same was to be done with the operational (horizontal) authority and responsibility. Because information was now computerized, it was no longer as necessary as in the past to have highly specialized partitioning of the work process. Certain responsibilities that had belonged to the production scheduling and methods departments could be assigned directly to operators in the lower levels of the organization.

However, within the confines of the plant, change had to proceed gradually. First, the departments had to be redirected toward large-scale tasks and then relieved of day-to-day responsibilities. This required creating direct, complementary partnerships between employees. This was the purpose of the production manager's pedagogical task.

Usually, the production manager had to get information from a group that was closer to the reality of the production units than he was. That being the case, however, there was no reason why he should have to follow the traditionally long official channels that turned information into orders and through that metamorphosis eliminated the motivating nature of the information.

Shouldn't there be direct relationships between transmitter and receiver to develop internal motivation within the group? Wasn't it more reasonable to put the production manager and the supervisor group in direct contact instead of subjecting the communication to hierarchical rules? Figure 18 illustrates his thinking on this point.

The production manager's communication model was, of course, more reasonable, quicker, and more motivating for the group, but habits still stood in the way, in some instances. The managers of the production scheduling and maintenance departments in particular clung to past practice while other department heads accepted that they could find legitimate spokespersons within the supervisor group. With these departments, the group managed to have participatory relationships, whereas in the past, the production units experienced conflict-based relationships.

This positive change was emphasized publicly one day by a member of management. That recognition from a decision maker helped to create new values of cooperation to replace the hierarchical values of times past.

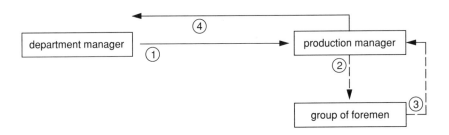

Figure 18.

Replacing Constraints with Motivating Responsibilities
(see Figure 4, quadrant 12)

Some people still think that group responsibility, based on the concerted efforts of the group members, cannot function effectively and that it results in chaos. Practice provides much evidence to the contrary.

During the long period of high growth, that conviction inhibited experiments not only at the lower levels of the organization, but also in the upper levels of management.

Under the favorable conditions of high growth, little importance was attached to the consequences (conflict and negative individualism) of this proliferation of constraints. As a result, little practical research was done to formulate other means of simultaneously ensuring good output, voluntary discipline, and creative individualism. The revival of the search for means of motivation accompanied the rapid change in world markets, which significantly heightened and intensified economic competition. That competition now requires a change in the way we employ human abilities.

Thus, managers are now beginning to accept the fact that output, work discipline, and quality of finished products can be ensured by means other than direct constraints. They are learning that being involved, having responsibility, and being consulted are better motivators than are external pressures from the management.

Raymond Dupont's group of skilled operators demonstrated that. Replacing constraints (fixed jobs, individual output, etc.) with collective output and group mechanisms (tandems, choice of tasks based on potential and abilities, etc.) even improved the former team's performance. The same situation was true in the supervisor group, where individual leadership gave way to concerted responsibility among the five members.

Of course, going from one to the other took time. But in one year, the new supports of group discipline and task distribution had been perfected. The new supports, which made it possible to draw on personal potential and abilities, were more productive than individual command.

What were the components of these new supports? At first, the basis of the supervisor group's operation was the tandem between Dupont and the curious foreman. The second important mechanism was the institution of a *daily consultation* about the goals to be achieved. This meeting increasingly accustomed employees to taking charge of problems with which they were familiar and for which they had the necessary skill.

Agreements with the departments (starting with the purchasing department) replaced the customary criticisms and protests with rules for consultation and joint analyses for the purpose of understanding the source of mutual errors.

The supervisor group's *direct involvement* in reviewing the daily and weekly machine shop schedule enhanced a sense of personal responsibility. Technical and organizational goals could be set each week in connection with problems encountered in carrying out the schedule. This motivated the group members to improve their results.

The disappearance of the middle levels of management was a stimulant. Problems could be handled wherever they occurred, by people who were familiar with them. This new situation created a sense of responsibility and streamlined the machine shop's relationships with operational departments.

The systematic consultation practiced by the new production manager involved the supervisor group members in important decisions. The observation and weekly review of dysfunctions in the machine shop put the group members into direct and constant contact with the coordinator.

The daily analysis of results proved effective because it explained the nature of the dysfunction and made it possible to set short-term goals.

Tandems, meetings (for scheduling or consultation), agreements with machine shop associates, the supervisor group's inclusion in reviewing the production schedule, consultation between the coordinator and the group, group inputs to the coordinator — all of these things bear no resemblance to the old constraints. The workers and supervisors instead experienced the new mechanisms as professional interest, personal usefulness, and an enhanced contribution to the efficiency of the machine shop.

Whereas the constraint system generated negative individualism, the supervisor group's new operational supports developed creative individualism, which was linked with internal motivation. Consequently, there was no vagueness or loss of authority. However, unlike the old constraints dictated by memos and very hierarchically organized relationships, the new mechanisms, which ensured conscious discipline, had to be tested. These mechanisms had to replace the old habits and overcome the consequences of negative individualism as well. That is what took time. It was a time for learning and perfecting.

Not until these mechanisms had proved effective were they officially institutionalized. As a result, for several months, the old operational structure was duplicated by a new, informal organization that was being tested. The workers learned to use the supports and mechanisms of that new organization. When the learning had yielded satisfactory results, the new informal organization could be institutionalized.

CHAPTER ELEVEN

The Overlapping of Complementary Functions

Special Action to Create Motivation
(see Figure 4, quadrants 12, 13)

This new operational structure, individualized and based on shared responsibility, was not easily accepted in the environment of the machine shop. Some of the functional departments regarded it for a long time with incomprehension and even hostility. Others viewed it with indifference ("another trick") or weariness.

There was also curiosity, however, particularly on the part of the purchasing department. During the breaking-in period, the foremen visibly interfered with the old operating rules and confused the department managers, who didn't have the customary hierarchical spokespersons as buffers. This situation can be illustrated by the following example.

The machine shop's relations with the maintenance department were especially complex and strained. The mechanics considered their jobs superior to other job categories, which irritated the production units and led them to seize opportunities to criticize maintenance. They felt that maintenance never arrived on site fast enough to repair breakdowns and that their service was rarely done well.

These criticisms annoyed the maintenance department's unit manager all the more, since he, who was an excellent handyman, was often obliged to do routine repairs. In practice, the slightest technical change in plant equipment was the responsibility of the design department. Because he was unable to employ his abilities, the maintenance unit manager was neither inspired nor internally motivated. He therefore became bitter and frustrated.

To escape this impasse, the machine shop's relationship with maintenance had to change. The production manager took the initiative. He asked the maintenance unit manager if he wanted to become a technical adviser to the foremen group. The unit manager accepted the offer, and the production manager got him a transfer. A little later, the dramatic change in his behavior amazed everyone. This man, who had been quarrelsome and never satisfied, knew how to be useful in his new role. He could now work according to his own inclination, preference, and actual competence. He was driven by internal motivation.

His case illustrates, at a higher level, the same lack of connection that often causes negative individualism in the front lines. His job, as it was defined and specialized in a maintenance activity, did not require his best abilities. As far as he was concerned, he did not have the patience necessary to do routine repairs without tiring. This situation resulted in a significant gap between his abilities and the job requirements, which led to behavior that was considered quarrelsome and disagreeable. The harmonious match between his abilities and the tasks of his new job overcame this negative individualism.

Overlapping Functions that Were Previously Separated
(see Figure 4, quadrants 12, 13)

A second example shows the positive effects of this process of assuming responsibility, which was fueled by the new technical adviser. In fact, he succeeded in creating harmony between the machine shop and the maintenance department and in transforming the design department as well. And he did so without quarrels or conflicts.

According to the procedure in effect — partially described above — the design department was responsible for devising technical modifications requested by production. Design change requests were filled out and routed through the various required levels of management. It was a long administrative process that dissociated the requesting party from the design. Since the requesting party frequently did not know precisely what the proper solution might be, the request was not always sufficiently clear. This lack of clarity was, moreover, a subject of ridicule ("they don't know what they want") among the design technicians. Such a situation did not create good relations with the production units.

There was no reciprocal assumption of responsibility between the design and production functions. Relations became strained rather than complementary, and tension triggered all kinds of emotional reactions. Instead of being motivated by the complementary nature of their roles, employees adopted negative attitudes toward people in the other functions.

This situation was a serious but nevertheless commonplace result of organizational inadequacy in the form of compartmentalized functions. The new technical adviser for the machine shop ultimately turned it around and replaced it with complementary roles. But implementing that kind of extremely motivating relationship ran counter to the old habits of task specialization. Consequently, in the beginning, he had to bypass certain steps in the administrative process.

To begin with, he wasn't satisfied to merely gather ideas from the machine shops to fill out design change requests, as was done before. He tested the ideas. He thoroughly studied the technical problem, deduced hypothetical solutions, questioned workers and foremen, and also conducted tests with the interested parties. In this way, design change requests were not only filled out quickly and precisely, but in many cases the design was already partially done. People could no longer dismiss the machine shop as ineffective.

The technical adviser even did profitability computations. If an idea seemed to be a good investment, he would take the design change requests directly to the design department. The manager of that department would protest. He wanted to draw up a file on each case and was not ready to handle change requests directly with the adviser. The production manager had to support the adviser's approach by stressing that the designs requested were the result of "prior selection."

The technical adviser didn't take all of the design change requests to the design department; that department could focus on "serious" and "important" requests. This was common sense, but the technical adviser upset everyone by reversing the order of the steps. According to customary procedure — established long ago during the high-growth period — even minor design change requests were reviewed by the design department. Consideration of their potential profitability came only later.

This irrational administrative approach had burdensome consequences. Designs later deemed "unprofitable" had to be stopped, resulting in a nearly 30 percent loss in the designers' work time. This was clearly a demotivating situation, and it became a subject of ridicule among designers and technicians.

In essence, the 30 percent loss in work time represented an overload for the plant and kept the design department from devoting itself to important tasks.

The technical adviser's action, which appropriated certain responsibilities from the design department and upset the customary administrative operating procedure, would make the activity of the designers and technicians *more profitable*. First, he introduced prior selection and evaluation into the process. Then he persisted in staying involved, following the design through, and implementing it. In so doing, he blended two functions that were previously strictly separated.

This second approach was much more rational. In the past, modifications were small-scale and often routine, but under the new economic situation, innovation was increasingly required, resulting in a significant increase in the number of design change requests. The technical adviser was therefore wise to introduce technical and financial selection into the process.

In addition, this manner of operation involved the group of machine shop foremen and even the handyman workers in the innovations, which created a motivating situation. It was the first step toward transferring certain administrative authority and responsibility to the supervisor group.

Such an approach was also advantageous for the design department, which saw its overload from the machining side decisively reduced. Under such circumstances, the technicians and designers themselves could be involved in the first stage of

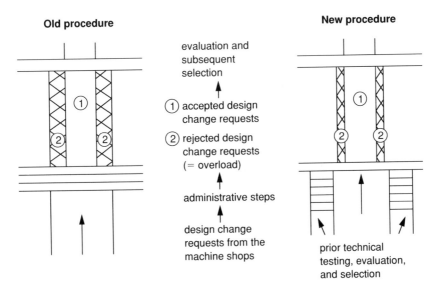

Figure 19.

the process, which enhanced the selection of ideas and created cooperative relationships with the machine shops.

The new approach was rejected at first by the design department because it blended tasks that traditionally had been separated, and it involved foremen and even workers in selecting ideas and technical testing. It brought designers and technicians into the process as well. Then, when the designs were already in process, it involved the machine shop foremen concerned.

For the design department manager, a well-reputed but rigid specialist, this was a "disturbance." From his point of view, no one knew any longer who had what responsibility in such a situation. The desire to separate and specialize the roles (to which he ascribed positive values by terming it "clarity") was, in his case, connected to the past. It related to his training and to the very specialized role that he had played during the long period of high growth. He literally derived his identity from that role. In the past, moreover, that was the surest way to establish a career. His internal motivation had turned into hierarchical ambition, which was ill-suited to the plant's new financial situation. As a result, he was transferred.

Multidimensional, Multi-actor Analyses
(see Figure 4, quadrants 11, 13)

The example of the design department was followed a little later by others. It was a way of revising the functions and reciprocal responsibilities that linked the machine shop to its partners.

In the past, the production areas "produced," but everything essential to that activity was handled by other functions in different departments. This system created operational authority and responsibility. In a computerized data environment, however, it lost a major part of its rationale for existence.

Fragmented responsibilities and specialized roles proved effective during the long period of mass production, but they were ill-suited to the competitive market situation. They restrained cooperation among potential partners and established blockages that regularly turned into misunderstandings and conflicts.

It was therefore necessary to transfer certain operational authority and responsibility to the front lines of the organization and to the middle-management level, precisely where practical problems had to be resolved. Establishing new rules of the game with the purchasing department and later establishing cooperation with the design department (based on overlapping roles) constituted the first steps in that direction.

In the old stable market context, each problem could be analyzed separately, isolated from numerous interactions. However, in the new economic situation, such a procedure was not profitable or rational. Various levels of management specialized in resolving particular types of problems, but the resolutions were not long-lasting because they did not address the causes within the operational structure.

The operational method of the new group of foremen was much more efficient. Problems were analyzed collectively in conjunction with all of their interactions. The results led to questions about establishing job positions (handled by the methods department), technical modifications of the equipment (handled by the design department), and even qualifications problems (which concerned personnel management).

The group analyzed all these correlations. However, their analysis required that the actors concerned — the operators, methods staff, personnel representatives, design department technicians, and so on — be involved in the interchanges.

Contrary to past procedure, in which analyses were specialized by subject and by the actor concerned, the new practice was a multidimensional, multi-actor analysis. This type of analysis required more time than specialized, one-dimensional analyses did, but it had the advantage of providing long-term resolutions for problems. In addition, this practice created a true network of exchange around the group of foremen.

Putting the problems back into the context of the pertinent interactions, studying their different aspects, and involving the actors in the analysis were ways of taking into account the complexity of competitive market demands and adapting the machine shop's organization to those demands.

The practice of multi-actor analyses, which had motivating effects, had other consequences as well. In fact, in the past, each department worked in accordance with its own methods and principles, without questioning whether its way of doing things was suitable to the manufacturing units.

The methods department, for example, established jobs according to its own criteria, such as specialization and technical fragmentation of production steps. The disturbances encountered in the machine shop and assembly shop teams, however, required a different concept, particularly task regrouping and job mobility. Multi-factor analyses enabled a gradual modification of the old criteria and formulation of new ones. The example of Raymond Dupont's team helped the department in this methodological change.

The same was true with the other departments. The result of all this was the development of complementary roles, accompanied by stimulating relationships.

Transferring Management Authority to the Front Lines
(see Figure 4, quadrants 11, 13)

Because of the rapid change effected in the machine shop environment, it became possible to revise some of the principal mainstays of the organization of work. In the past, these organizational factors, above all, had to reinforce the basic principles of the operational structure — the specialization of tasks and the hierarchical organization of relationships.

In the ongoing change, however, these demotivating factors were reoriented to encourage employees to adapt their abilities and cooperate with one another.

The principal factors involved were information, issue resolution, respective rights and obligations, and the distribution of responsibilities. Before the transformation of the machine shop, all of these factors were in the service of the organizational chart, weighing it down with hierarchical relationships.

Formerly, the production manager personally received the mail and the principal information concerning production units. He distributed it each morning to the production unit managers, who did likewise with the head foreman. In the context of a very hierarchical organization, this was a ritualistic and demotivating situation because information created a feeling of dependency.

Problems were not analyzed and handled at the level directly concerned, but rather at the highest levels of management. As a result, these levels took on a critical, authoritarian attitude. The operational departments knew this quite well, and they therefore developed the reflex of always addressing their questions to the highest possible level of management.

In the past, respective rights and obligations were not distributed according to practical needs but rather according to each person's place in the organizational hierarchy. They consequently reinforced subordinate relationships. The foremen could not sign orders to replace a broken or worn-out tool; they needed the signature of the production unit manager. If machines were to be modified, the unit manager had sole authority with respect to design and budget appropriations, regardless of the amount of money involved. He was also the sole spokesperson for the design department. When an employee had to leave the plant, the foreman filled out a form and had it signed by the production unit chief, even if the latter didn't know the worker.

Finally, responsibilities, which were closely related to the assignment of rights and obligations, were a function of each person's place in the organizational hierarchy — not his or her knowledge, skills, abilities, or the tasks for which he was responsible.

The new economic situation was increasingly intolerant of the hierarchical distribution of information, responsibilities, and authority to handle problems and sign off on forms. In the past, when production was still steady and disturbances were rare and routine, the intensely hierarchical aspect of the organizational factors had few negative effects. But as market demands diversified, the situation changed. At first, the demands were regarded as "disturbances" because the production units lacked flexibility and could not meet them effectively. When the disturbances would not disappear, various levels of the management hierarchy specialized in resolving those special problems.

This remedial tendency was inevitable because management had not altered the individual output system or the practice of creating highly specialized jobs at the lower levels of the organization. Since the operators could not adapt at their level to new market demands, it was up to the corporate hierarchy to do so. In this way, the management apparatus became a true "remedial instrument" by necessity.

Raymond Dupont's "underground initiative" broke this cycle. In the collective output system adopted by his team, employees could alter the rigid distribution of operations, obligations, and even responsibilities. The departure of the old production manager cleared the way for extending the new system to other teams. Finally, the flattening of the management hierarchy "desubordinated" the various organizational factors. From then on, changes in schedules and priorities were handled directly — following consultation — by a member of the group of foremen. Information could be routed directly to whoever needed it.

Problems were also handled at the level of employee involvement. Technical modifications of equipment were designed directly by the technical advisor in close collaboration with the job and the foreman concerned.

The distribution of responsibilities, rights, and obligations also departed from the old hierarchical context. Filling in orders and signatures were no longer acts of subordination or hierarchical superiority, but rather acts required in order to accomplish various tasks. Taking a tool from the store room became a right assigned to the task of executing the schedule and therefore to the operator. The teams managed their tools, as well as the necessary budget for any replacements. And those who feared abuses came to realize that the new distribution of responsibilities led to far fewer abuses than in the old system.

That profound internal transformation and the desubordination of organizational factors were, of course, observed and commented on by those around the machine shop. They were discussed in other production units and in operational departments as well. Discussing a change, especially when the results underscored its importance and need, awakened curiosity in those around the machine shop. It also made it easier for the experiment to penetrate other work areas. Without that profound influence, the machine shop's technical adviser could not have triggered the developmental process in the design department.

CHAPTER TWELVE

Transferring Labor Relations Authority to the Front Lines

When an experiment is observed and its results and problems are commented on, the situation becomes clearer. Positions become crystallized. Those who are "in favor" stay more informed and even try to conduct experiments in their own work area. Others pave the way for future action. Those who are "against" must find arguments, magnify errors, and interpret the results unfavorably. But they are also forced to compare their arguments with the facts.

That continual process of clarification prevented rumors and gross distortions in Raymond Dupont's plant. Curiosity triumphed over skepticism.

The sole exception in that regard was the area of labor relations authority, which was shared specifically by various units in the employee relations department and the labor representatives. Resistance was stronger in this area than in the others.

The supervisor group evolved quickly. Eventually, its members acquired knowledge and experience with group work, in which roles must be complementary. They also succeeded in penetrating the specialized areas of the different departments. Gradually, functions overlapped, and certain operational powers and responsibilities were transferred to the group level. Due to this reform, management could redirect the departments toward designing major innovations.

The same tendency was also observed in the area of management authority and responsibility because the disappearance of two middle-management levels had removed obstacles.

On the other hand, progress was slow in the area of personnel management, where authority and responsibility were still assigned to units within the employee relations office and to the roles performed by labor representatives.

The long period of high growth had created not only operational (horizontal) and management (vertical) authority and responsibility, but also labor relations authority and responsibility involving personnel management. This was because the intensive specialization of jobs dictated a highly uniform, impersonal type of management.

The unions collaborated in formulating the various management methods, even when that collaboration was invariably linked to labor conflict. That was their area of interest; this system, which ignored individuals and their abilities, had serious labor consequences that formed the very basis for their grievance-mongering role.

After each major labor conflict, the system of job qualification, pay, evaluation, and promotion was reworked accordingly. Since the number of minor grievances continued to rise, the labor relations units of the personnel department increased staff.

The more the employees received enhanced training on the front lines, the more their jobs (which never changed or evolved) generated negative attitudes. And insofar as dissatisfaction intensified, it was also necessary to increase managerial staff to put out the small fires that smoldered throughout the production units.

There was no way out of this situation. Disputes could break out at any time, since personal problems were not taken into consideration in an impersonal system.

Substitutions and time standards, in particular, were constant sources of conflict. A supervisor who needed to move someone to substitute for an absent employee had to take precautions. If the substitute was more highly qualified (through professional testing) than the job to be filled required, he could demand a substitution bonus. If, on the other hand, the job was ranked higher than the employee, the management would criticize the foreman if there was a machining error.

In other instances, errors and mistakes were usually "explained" as a function of the time allocated — the time frame was "too tight." Since the standard times were objective and impersonal, they didn't take into account the abilities that determined individual time. The same amount of time allocated could be sufficient for some and too little for others, depending on whether a worker was fast or slow, superficial or thorough. If there was a dispute, however, the time frame always proved to be "too tight."

During that long period, the foremen found themselves in an ambiguous situation. They had to comply with timekeeping, even though they had no responsibility for how time was allocated. If workers initiated a grievance, they were criticized by the labor representatives because they represented management in the production unit.

Under such circumstances, personal problems systematically became interpersonal conflicts and then labor conflicts. A foreman who was criticized would appeal to his superiors, while the labor representatives would threaten to stop the work of the entire production unit. If a strike was actually triggered, the unions were assured of support from the other production units in order to be in a good bargaining position. The outcome of negotiations always depended on the balance of power.

But it was clearly not the foremen who handled the negotiations, or even the department in charge of timekeeping. Instead, it was the personnel manager or his assistant. It was, therefore, a typical situation in which roles were determined by the criterion of specialization, which fragmented responsibilities and made it easy for disputes to turn into labor conflicts.

The system was demotivating for the members of the managerial staff and detrimental to the plant. The impossibility of resolving personal problems literally compelled collective grievances related to pay increases, general bonuses, changes in qualification, and so forth.

This mechanism was obviously costly. It increased unproductive costs without providing any offsets. In the past, such costs were absorbed by uniformly high growth, but in the competitive market situation they necessarily increased the selling price.

The transformation of minor disputes into labor conflicts was, however, a prestige factor for labor representatives and, to a certain extent, even for the employee relations office, which performed a savior role in each instance. But ultimately, the most dangerous element of this long-standing practice was its conditioning effect. After several decades of such practices, labor representatives could no longer imagine their role in the plant in any other way.

The front-line managers, who had no real responsibility in this area, were accustomed to withdrawing in the event of conflict and conceding to the labor organizations. Under these circumstances, efforts to strengthen the labor management staff with attorneys were only a remedial measure, since the source of the conflicts was usually the impersonal aspect of the labor representation system. Personal problems could be resolved only by altering bonuses, pay scales, qualifications, and allocated time.

Raymond Dupont found his solution by secretly creating collective output within his team, which made it possible to resolve personal issues without conflict. After that system was extended to other machine shops, and particularly after certain operational and management responsibilities were transferred to the supervisor group level, it was no longer possible to delay labor management reforms. In this area too, significant authority and responsibility had to be transferred to create a comprehensive sharing of accountability.

Nevertheless, the transfer was hard to effect because of long-standing tradition, and also because the foremen did not yet have enough experience and knowledge in this area. The management therefore decided to create two "labor relations advisers" in the machine shop, as a first step. The two people were chosen from among volunteers in the personnel department. Their role was to inform and advise the supervisors about the various provisions of labor law and collective bargaining agreements.

The goal was to transfer even local negotiations to the members of the group. Hence, the supervisor group learned to hold health and safety meetings and began to deal directly with problems raised by labor representatives.

The new practice disconcerted the unions, which were accustomed to negotiating with top management. At the outset, they protested against transferring labor relations authority and responsibility to the supervisor group. They were also surprised that, from then on, they were unable to turn personal problems into labor conflicts.

First, in the context of collective output, the employees themselves resolved most of the assignment problems. In the event of a dispute, supervisors always looked for concrete responses. They involved in their analysis not only the people concerned, but also the other members of the team.

When the output in a particular job was insufficient, group discussion usually revealed that the job had requirements that the operator could not meet. On the other hand, the employee also had abilities that the job did not call for. And so, it was necessary to modify the distribution of tasks.

In each instance, precise analysis made it possible to find the source of the personal problem. Disputes about qualifications disappeared gradually because, in the context of collective output, the members of a team knew quite well who was capable of what.

In monthly meetings, they also evaluated complexity of tasks, new problems, and "services rendered." If someone disagreed, he had the option of providing proof to the contrary. He could also appeal to the production manager and the labor representatives.

These evaluation meetings and dispute procedures prevented hidden conflicts and erroneous judgments. They made it possible to measure not only each person's ability at the time, but also individual development and progress. This became the basis for pay increases that account for not only direct machining work but also the employees' participation in other areas, such as waste reduction, quality of machined parts, various supplementary jobs, observations, proposals, innovations, and so forth. The broadening of the evaluation criteria made it possible to determine the real input of employees much more accurately than the sole quantitative criterion of individual output.

These new evaluation criteria, evaluation meetings, and dispute procedures completely overturned the union's former customs and practices. Labor representatives attended the meetings, of course, but they could no longer turn personal problems into labor conflicts. They were bewildered by the new situation, for it required them to take on new roles.

They nevertheless could have found in the machine shop a field for experimentation in which to formulate roles that matched the internal changes in the teams and the new economic environment.

The individualization of jobs, of the teams' organization, and of issue resolution in fact required considerable monitoring to clarify and implement the mechanisms of the new operational structure. Such mechanisms — meetings, the right to appeal in the event of disputes, new evaluation criteria — were already taking shape, and some were even becoming standard procedure. However, more work was needed in this area, and the labor representatives had an important role to perform there. Some of them who were less conditioned than the others accepted the principle of cooperation and thereby profoundly altered their relationship with the teams.

In a medium-sized company, a certain amount of labor relations authority and responsibility can be transferred to the front-line management quickly. But in Raymond Dupont's plant, where tradition was strong and there was stubborn resistance to change, it required a gradual process.

It is no longer unusual to see companies, particularly small and medium-sized ones, transfer almost all such authority and responsibility to the lowest management level. Hiring, employee evaluation (with employee input), promotions, pay increases, and union negotiations are examples of the types of authority and responsibility sometimes transferred.

Once certain administrative and management powers have been reassigned, such transfers create full responsibility, which is motivating. They also make it possible to increase employee participation to a significant degree and to deal effectively with the practical problems of a competitive market.

PART FIVE

Creative Individualism: A New Organizational Principle

The change in the world economy that began in the early 1970s compels businesses and nations to adapt to the new demands of the competitive market. This adaptation occurred rapidly in some countries, while in others it has been slow and painful. The more adaptable countries reoriented economically:

- Instead of gambling on cheap labor, businesses innovated to increase their production capacity.
- Instead of restricting imports, they developed exports.
- Instead of implementing remedial mechanisms to achieve internal harmony, they developed mechanisms for labor-management compromise and participation.

In these countries the advent of profound technological and economic change did not produce a shock. In other countries, by contrast, it produced an internal socioeconomic crisis, particularly with regard to skills and the operational structure of business and government.

Such a domestic crisis occurs independently of the political sensibilities of established regimes and governments. Above all, it has to do with level of skill, not ideology. How domestic economies adapt to the new competitive market imperatives now depends principally on the operational structure of businesses and government.

Governments do not create wealth, but they do redistribute it. Optimally, they can use stimulating redistribution techniques. They can, in fact, accelerate the development of new operational structures or maintain outmoded rigid organizational structures.

If use of the latter is currently declining, it is mainly because of the menacing impact of competition. Raymond Dupont's plant succeeded in correcting its technological lag through advantageous government loans, but that did not shield it from new dangers. The successful machine shop experiment, on the other hand, increased productivity without new investment. In applying the experiment more generally, two levels of the corporate hierarchy were eliminated, and the process of overlapping the functions of the machine shop and the operational departments was backed by management. What common sense and labor conflicts could not achieve during the long period of high growth, the competitive market dictated in the space of a few years.

Within the framework of an individualized organization, the nature of professional relationships changed. Before, they were based on hierarchical subordination and represented additional constraints and barriers for those performing production processes. The frustrating nature of such barriers and constraints lent importance to the union movement, which was also used to resolve technical and organizational problems. Such labor relationships, which were a privileged avenue of communication, were a source of prestige for labor representatives, but they did nothing to change the specialized and demotivating nature of jobs. In fact, labor representatives used the balance of power, which had been in their favor in an unsaturated market, to obtain additional across-the-board benefits rather than to free up jobs.

The successful experiment reestablished within the plant the importance of direct professional relationships, which were no longer fragmented by scattered powers and responsibilities. To resolve the various problems of the production units, there was no longer a need to appeal to the union movement. The persons affected could be contacted directly.

The resulting change was profound. Before, employees had to adapt to an organization that rigorously selected abilities. Barriers and constraints prohibited them from escaping the narrow confines of their work. By contrast, in the framework of an individualized organization, the operational structure of departments and production units had to adapt to internal motivations and personal abilities.

The machine shop went a long way in that direction, but it could not go all the way, at least for the time being. Resistance to change still existed.

Applying the principle of creative individualism opened up possibilities that could not yet be fully explored. Those possibilities, however, are now being explored in small companies, where skill-based competition mechanisms are being applied. In these companies, which are not handicapped by a ponderous, complex organization, the operational structure has a competitive nature that responds effectively to market demands.

This new phase in individualized organization (which can also be called "competitive organization") makes it possible to take advantage of internal motivation to the maximum extent. However, implementing such an organization presupposes an extensive behavioral development in order to eliminate the last traces of resistance to change.

CHAPTER THIRTEEN

Individualized Organization: A Broad Potential for Change

Creative Individualism: A New Organizational Principle
(see Figure 4, quadrant 22)

In many market segments, intensive specialization of jobs and functions no longer can respond to competitive market demands or social and cultural advances. The consistency of the old rigid operational structure was specifically guaranteed by various constraints, but an individualized organization is driven by internal motivation. In Raymond Dupont's machine shop, such motivation was sustained by mechanisms for cooperation, consultation, and the promotion of complementary roles.

In that area of work, the new structure now rests not on a ponderous organizational structure, but rather on a multitude of small groups that closely overlap each other. As a result, there is much less risk of seeing professional motivation turn into hierarchical ambition. However, the new structure also restores administrative, management, and labor powers to the front lines.

Dupont's successful experiment turned into an organizational model for the entire work area and even for surrounding departments because management finally understood that in the new economic context, one of its most important roles is to recognize local innovative experiments and efficient employees. After that, the coordination function paves the way for strategic action and guides development.

Most of the machine shop's partners likewise became quickly involved in the process of change. The new consistency of the organization of work, based on the principle of employee motivation, therefore gained ground.

Furthermore, since financial outcomes confirmed the efficiency of the new operational structure after a brief break-in period, management favored extending it to all manufacturing areas. In this phase of the program, the machine shop's production manager performed the same role with respect to his colleagues as the foreman did earlier in forming the supervisor group.

Progress was rapid. The considerable improvement in the machine shop's costs (through small improvements and reduced waste) and the flexibility of the organization of work offered results that were more convincing than those produced through customary remedial means.

It is, of course, necessary to know employees in order to facilitate full use of their abilities and potential. Supervisors can implement a variety of means in that respect — surveys, personal interviews, improvised situations that test the value of work methods, tandems, and small groups within teams, varying their composition to see who works well with whom and what knowledge and abilities complement each other.

This is a role that many managers perform intuitively because they know that pure knowledge, symbolized by a degree or a professional test, is not enough to be effective. Effectiveness is proved every day on the job.

To create a source of conflict in a group, one need only put a slow worker beside a fast worker, a regular worker with an erratic worker, an analytical mind with a mind with a gift for synthesis, a careful worker with a bold worker. In the old system of individual output, these differences in abilities were always a source of tension and misunderstandings.

In a collective output system, that diversity can become complementary, provided that effective human relations techniques and mechanisms are carefully formulated. This complementarity is one of the main functions of a group, whether of workers or supervisors.

Analyses lead to the shaping of personal histories, a kind of summary of an individual's knowledge, experience, and abilities. The supervisors compare these summaries to the work load of the team involved, the nature of the operations, the diversity of the tasks, special requirements, etc. The operations to be carried out are analyzed accordingly, not only technically (the knowledge criterion), but also behaviorally (the abilities criterion) and in terms of relationships (the group mechanisms criterion).

Within the framework of a collective output system, just a few months of training were sufficient for the machine shop operators to begin applying these three criteria on their own and for the distribution of tasks to show the greatest possible conformity with internal motivation and personal abilities.

Once they had made progress in that direction, the traditional emotional reactions gradually disappeared. The jealousies, animosities, susceptibilities, bad dispositions, and poor outlooks that had been regarded as innate gave way to careful agreements and collaborations. Customary opinions and criticisms had no further reason to exist, since slowness was no longer a defect. It was, rather, a quality that was perfectly suited to certain tasks.

Freed of the old constraints and criticisms from the corporate hierarchy, team members could devote themselves to tasks that were suited to their knowledge as well as their motivation. This fundamental change improves financial outcomes.

The Developmental Process in the Machine Shop
(see Figure 4, quadrants 11, 12)

The developmental process was practically complete with respect to the teams' internal organization and work load allocation, once middle managers were eliminated. Overlapping functions between the machine shop and the operational departments were relatively much improved, thanks to the activity of the technical adviser and the production manager.

On the other hand, personnel management and labor relations authority and responsibility were slow to change. There was also a lag in participation with regard to technical and sales/marketing functions. The machine shop had negligible participation in these areas because these were considered the most prestigious functions in the plant.

The sales office had grown very quickly and held a leveraged position in relation to its counterparts, particularly manufacturing. It was not easy to persuade its staff to consult with foremen or inform the teams so that they could understand the source of scheduling changes and express ideas on quality.

Product improvement and launching new products were also sources of prestige in the plant, and technical employees did not willingly share that prestige. Nevertheless, it turned out that, in many instances, small improvements originated by the manufacturing teams contained ideas that led to the design of major improvements at little additional cost. Modifications that were implemented on the basis of theory, without accounting for the equipment's technical constraints, always required an investment. It was not easy to convince people that it was advantageous for the technical and research units to work on small improvements and therefore have direct relationships with the teams.

In fact, progress was achieved in these two areas only when corporate management supported the process. Here too, as in the other situations, allies had to be found in the departments concerned, and the efficiency of overlapping responsibilities had to be demonstrated.

The regrouping and overlapping of responsibilities in the places where most practical problems arose gave supervisors additional means of fully using personal abilities and potential. It signaled the completion of a long, difficult, but inevitable transformation of the competitive position of the plant.

Expanding the New System from the Bottom Up
(see Figure 4, quadrants 12, 13)

Such a profound change, experienced in the machine shop before being expanded to other manufacturing areas, overturned the idea of professional categories as well as relationships between the supervisory level and other functions. In the past, these relationships were subordinate, since responsibilities were fragmented, and each fragment was assigned a value related to an increasing portion of power within the corporate hierarchy.

With the regrouping of practical responsibilities and the overlapping of functions, relationships between internal partners changed. From then on, they were based on complementary roles, which proved to be stimulating.

This change was ultimately imposed throughout the plant for practical reasons. In the old unsaturated market, products had a long life cycle. Demand remained high, and production of the same models could continue for years. Under such circumstances, the upper levels of management focused on current problems because the future was not pressing. They had their portion of responsibility for the daily work of the departments and production units. Thus, the relative value of these everyday problems organized themselves hierarchically according to the level of management at which they were resolved.

Consequently, foremen, who worked directly with workers, had no responsibility in the various areas of personnel management, in the resolution of interpersonal and labor conflicts, in the area of equipment budgets, or in the relationships between their production units and other areas of manufacturing. Thus, problems that were often simple and routine gained exceptional importance because resolving them was the responsibility of a higher level of management.

There were many dangers in such a practice, which was a function of vertical specialization of roles. It demotivated supervisors, who were, nevertheless, in the best position to study and resolve the various situations. The number of little problems identified tended to increase considerably because of improved professional training, but jobs did not evolve correspondingly and remained as specialized as before. The partial saturation of the market accelerated the process, so little problems and disturbances of all kinds became intrusive. It became impossible to maintain the practice of vertical specialization.

The last stage in the process was related to substantially heightened competition. Within a few years, product life was seriously reduced. Thereafter, it became necessary to introduce a new, or at least considerably improved model, every year. And the production manager, who in the past focused completely on the short term, now had to be concerned above all with practical preparation for the annual introduction of new models. He had to provide for technical modification of equipment, reshuffling of jobs, training of operators, and other activities.

Everyday problems lost much of their hierarchical importance. Under the new circumstances, they simply became a burden. Therefore, it was critical to regroup and entrust them to the supervisor level, which was in the best position to handle them. That freed the production manager to serve as a coordinator who focused on medium-term problems.

This was even more true for management, which in the past was also swamped by everyday problems. In the context of a competitive market, forecasting, market research, analysis of technical and market data, and preparation of a bold but realistic strategy acquired enormous importance, and it was management's role to take responsibility for such functions.

Of course, prosperous companies in a market niche where economic activity is favorable can postpone regrouping and overlapping the various powers and responsibilities at the lowest levels of the organization. This actually happens in certain instances, in which companies maintain the hierarchical ordering of dealing with small problems and hire specialists for the tasks intrinsic to the competitive market, or they entrust those tasks to outside organizations, since the management function is not available to attend to the future.

However, such solutions have serious consequences. They prevent intensive utilization of skills because they require the more highly trained employees to attend to problems from which they are removed and whose nature and significance they cannot grasp precisely. Such a role is demotivating. It stifles the spirit of initiative and literally obligates the people involved to devote themselves to hierarchical ambition.

Despite their high cost, such solutions remain possible in certain market sectors where economic activity is favorable and competition is not yet intense. But this was not true in the case of Raymond Dupont's plant, where a change in authority and responsibility had become essential to enhance the spirit of initiative and develop creative individualism at all levels.

It certainly would have been preferable for strategic action to start at the highest levels and then penetrate the functional departments and production units. But as is so often true, a course of action cannot always apply the quickest and most rational methodology because circumstances are not favorable. Sometimes action is set in motion when a strong manager paves the way for it. In the case of the plant, that manager was the machine shop foreman.

CHAPTER FOURTEEN

Competition Based on Skill and Ability

The Vestiges of Resistance to Change
(see Figure 3, quadrant 21; Figure 4, quadrant 23)

Could Raymond Dupont's plant go still further in using creative individualism? Had the unblocking of jobs, the overlapping of functions, and transfer of powers and responsibilities reached their limits? Was there still more unexplored potential for more intensively using personal abilities and knowledge?

Such potential did in fact exist, but tapping it depended on a major behavioral evolution. Even after many constraints disappeared, and even after several reforms were implemented, behavior was still partially conditioned by the past. In fact, attitudes and thinking may remain unchanged for a long time, even after their material and organizational justifications have disappeared. Attitudes do not change automatically; quite often, conscious action is required.

Such was the case at Dupont's plant. The successful experiment locally eliminated most of the blockages. Outmoded constraints disappeared, and responsibilities that were regarded as sources of prestige within the corporate hierarchy were integrated into the jobs of operators and supervisors.

Where, then, are the limits? A simple example reveals the answer. When the old production manager of the machine shop was to be replaced, a member of management put forward Raymond Dupont's name as a possible successor.

That recommendation caused deep discomfort throughout the plant. Although the merits of the successful experiment had been recognized, limits to its application suddenly appeared.

The limits were emotional in nature. The need to extend the foreman's results throughout the work area and even its surrounding environment had been acknowledged. And it was also agreed that such an extension required a skilled coordinator who had the necessary qualifications.

In that case, why not entrust the job to Raymond Dupont? He had proved his skill as an organizer and had a strong personality and an analytical, experimental mind.

But thinking in the plant still conformed to old criteria and principles, and emotional reactions were sustained by a scale of values and considerations that precluded skill-based competition for promotions.

As a result, although people recognized Dupont's strengths, they objected that he was "only a supervisor," that to make him "fit in" he would have to go through extensive training, and then he was already "over fifty," that he didn't have a degree, and so forth.

A comparison of the principal requirements for the coordinator job with the foreman's ability and qualifications would have resulted in a match. But no such appraisal took place. Competition for the job did not develop in the form of a specific evaluation but rather according to traditional principles and criteria such as rules, age, and education.

Such criteria certainly indicate that a person has acquired knowledge, but they cannot guarantee effectiveness. The old machine shop production manager had a university degree and was a trained engineer. He nevertheless was ineffective in his job. His personality and abilities did not meet the requirements of his position.

Raymond Dupont was handicapped in terms of theoretical knowledge, but his strong personality and experimental mind made him a perfect candidate for a coordinator position. In this plant, however, skill-based competition was still supplanted by traditional requirements, a legacy of the long period of high growth.

Competition based on skill and ability did already exist, in the teams and the supervisor group. Even in those two cases, however, there were certain limits.

The inquisitive employee from Dupont's old team, the one who used to wander around picking up information, made a small improvement one day. The idea came to him as he lingered in the assembly shop, observing how the different parts were used. He realized that a small machining modification would make the assemblers' work easier and would enable them to eliminate many costly defects.

It was such a good idea that the design department adopted it immediately. Raymond Dupont did propose to the management that his inquisitive worker be partially relieved of machining work in order to walk around in the assembly shops. His proposal was rejected, however, and the matter ended there.

From an organizational point of view, Dupont's suggestion represented a breakthrough for facilitating technical innovations. The idea was to expand the activities of the machine shop downstream to the assembly shop in the form of application control — verifying that the technical problems of assembly were adequately considered by the machinists. Useful modifications in technical designs and machining could then be made in response to problems encountered by the customers — the assembly workers.

The proposal was rejected because creating such a job for the inquisitive worker would combine the roles of worker and technician — a frequent occurrence in small companies — and would complicate personnel management.

There was a reason that no such job was included in the classification system. In the context of rigid organization, where tasks were compartmentalized and specialized, there was no need for such a position. But under more competitive market conditions, these combined occupations and jobs could help eradicate compartmentalization and speed up the innovation process.

The introduction of such jobs certainly threatened to call into question the old classification system and complicate personnel management, at least in the short term. In the long term, it appeared inevitable that occupations and jobs would adapt to competitive market imperatives.

Raymond Dupont found himself in a similar situation. He could perform effectively as a "skill detective" by partially leaving the confines of the supervisor group. His facility for observation and experimentation enabled him to make a quick analysis of the actors and to find workers who were capable of stimulating localized action in their work areas.

However, in this instance as well, performing this role would require the combination of two functions, which was not customary at the plant. Dupont's dual skills were eventually acknowledged, but only after much hesitation and with obvious discomfort; after all, how could management entrust him with such a role if he had no formal credentials? According to plant procedure, he needed extensive training.

Competition Based on Skill and Ability
(see Figure 4, quadrants 11, 12)

Some companies, especially small ones, are now sweeping away the final resistance to change. The big difference between them and Dupont's plant lies in the attitude of management. In small companies, managers' thinking is no longer encumbered with the ideas and principles of an outmoded scale of values. They systematically apply the criteria of creative individualism and competition based on skill and ability.

In fact, they know that degrees, rules, professional status, age, and seniority are only indicators that provide information and probabilities of success but must be actually confirmed in terms of the specific requirements of the work. This is particularly true because many positions of responsibility require a certain type of personality, abilities, and motivation. Theoretical knowledge is certainly useful, but in these cases it is secondary. Such positions are therefore filled through competition on the basis of skills and abilities.

Given the fact that human resources represent a major key to financial success in the competitive market, every effort should be made to achieve the closest possible compatibility between positions of responsibility and personal abilities. This compatibility, which is often random, ambivalent, or even antagonistic under rigid operating conditions, becomes powerful in an individualized organization where the criterion of skill-based competition is applied.

A measurement of the degree of compatibility (very low, low, somewhat high, very high) between personal qualifications and a company's requirements for positions of responsibility will give an accurate idea of the nature and intensity of employee motivation.

Before corrective action was taken at Dupont's plant, there was low compatibility (sometimes very low) in the job matches. This was true not only in the front lines and supervisory ranks but also at the highest levels of management. The case of the old production manager was the rule rather than the exception.

After the rapid evolution described earlier, compatibility between jobs and the people who held them became somewhat high in the machine shop and its environs. But it could have become very high. That maximum compatibility is the objective of companies striving to apply creative individualism as an organizational criterion.

Such companies abandon the long-standing practice of managing jobs, occupations, professional categories, careers, conflicts, and seniority. This kind of management was the basis for stabilization and standardization in the context of rigid organization. A competitive market, however, requires risk-taking (not stabilization), unleashing of creative individualism (not standardization), and adaptation of jobs to personal potential and abilities (not unequal "equality").

Will setting aside a well-honed management system and applying the criterion of skill-based competition result in chaos? Such actions clearly upset the customs and principles of stability and the old scale of grievance-based values. They also create new evaluation and human relations mechanisms, as illustrated by the formation of the supervisor group in Dupont's machine shop. However, in this last instance, the authority and responsibility granted could have gone much further, as it now has in many dynamic small firms and "subsidiary" companies.

Opportunities Generated by Creative Individualism
(see Figure 4, quadrants 11, 12)

How can a company exploit the extensive opportunities created by an individualized organization? Action is usually taken in three areas:

1. *Jobs:*
   - The creation of units with complementary operations, to escape the narrow confines of specialization.
   - The creation of overall responsibility by assigning to job positions indispensable practical authority, duties, and responsibilities, which may be horizontal (operational), vertical (management), or related to labor relations.

- Making all jobs, including high-level jobs with broad responsibilities, open and up for grabs by applying the principle of skill-based competition in all cases.
- Avoiding job stabilization and allowing jobs to remain subject to change in accordance with the needs of the economic environment. Certain jobs may quickly take on special importance; others may disappear or be modified depending on changes in the work load.

2. *Individuals:*
   - Seeking the best match between job requirements and personal potential and abilities.
   - Eliminating constraints that hinder the unleashing of internal motivation.
   - Encouraging initiative and risk-taking.
   - Developing open minds.
   - Assimilating individuals into groups, which are often assigned substantial powers and responsibilities.

3. *Work groups:*
   - Creating a high degree of complementarity between jobs.
   - Replacing specialized, hierarchically ordered roles with collective responsibility.
   - Starting with basic groups, and forming "clusters" (units) that combine operational and functional groups.
   - Placing these clusters horizontally or vertically, according to practical needs, by superimposing them on each other.
   - Assigning the groups and clusters (combinations of groups) substantial authority and responsibility in financial and labor relations matters, e.g., distribution of the work load, product quality control, local

purchasing authority, establishing wage levels (with the framework of extensive budget autonomy), hiring, choice of managers and supervisors, etc.

Such rights and responsibilities sometimes require complete transfer of long-standing management, operational, and labor relations authority and responsibility to these work groups.

An analysis of Raymond Dupont's machining area shows that it is now quite advanced in terms of jobs, but the opening up of supervision and coordination opportunities is still insufficient. In terms of individuals, the results are good, but there remains extensive untapped potential.

Finally, progress is still insufficient at the group level. The supervisor group and the coordinator position do share management responsibilities. The functional departments and the supervisor group overlap each other considerably on the horizontal level. However, there has not been enough progress in the area of financial (budgetary) and labor relations responsibilities, which are necessary for the work groups.

This new dynamism dictates that the shop floor should have extensive autonomy in the area of purchasing authority and personnel management. It is a major reform that requires eliminating the last vestiges of resistance to change.

The computerization of information and management now makes it possible to progress quickly along those lines. There is no longer any technical resistance to change. The authority of the departments and divisions over the units can therefore be relaxed. This authority can even be transformed into computerized production scheduling, technical and market information systematically distributed to the departments and production units, and advisory roles.

If autonomy within units within a company is achieved, then authority and responsibility can be transferred to the three levels cited above, and the criterion of skill-based competition can be fully applied.

This criterion can be applied to individuals as well as work groups. Competition on the basis of skill and ability can assume a collective aspect. Machine shop teams now have a say in the assignment of supervisors. One of the old foremen was thus replaced by someone else proposed by the team members. But the same competition criterion is not yet applied in connection with the coordinator, who is appointed by management.

In some small companies that are more highly evolved in organizational terms, using internal motivation no longer encounters behavioral resistance to change. In these rare companies, work groups apply the skill-based competition criterion. They choose supervisors and, through them, even high-level managers.

They can also make their own counterproposals to investment plans by employing the skill-based competition criterion. The same goes for staffing, hiring, and assignments. Since members of these groups know their practical constraints much better than upper managers do, competition works in their favor.

In highly progressive instances, application of the new competition criterion completely replaces old subordinate relationships, the old power of the corporate hierarchy, and the old rules for distributing authority and responsibility. Such instances therefore illustrate how effective operational mechanisms can minimize the number of errors caused by traditional decision making.

Such mechanisms make it possible to visualize the future structure of a workplace such as Dupont's machine shop. It will bear no resemblance to rigid, highly organized operational structures (see Figure 20).

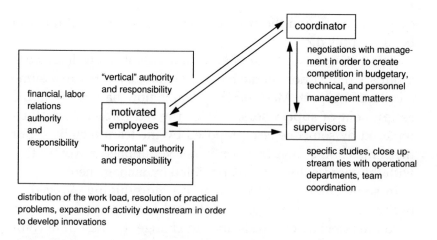

Figure 20.

Can the New System Be Extended to Labor Representation?
(see Figure 4, quadrant 13)

There is a place for labor representation in an individualized operational structure that grants major responsibility (even financial and budgetary) to individuals and work groups — but with the proviso that such representation also apply the criterion of skill-based competition.

The long period of high growth, with its regularly growing demand and long product life, determined the roles and functions of the various professional categories. The future was not pressing or threatening, the short term was of particular concern, and short-term problems were divided among different levels of management and the operational departments.

In the context of an unsaturated market, growth was extensive and quantitative. More machines were purchased, and more personnel were hired. During this extended period of time, the technological evolution of the means of production occurred without dramatic upheavals, and inadequacies were mitigated by a highly specialized use of personnel.

During this period, a rigid organization of work was supposed to ensure uniform, stable production and had no need for a spirit of initiative or creative individualism. Moreover, numerous constraints made it difficult to draw on personal potential and abilities. For this reason, dissatisfaction and a feeling of frustration drove employees, even those at the higher levels, to seek compensatory gratification. They found it in hierarchical ambition, interests outside of work, and, very often, grievance-mongering activities, which were the origin of the practice of adopting enhanced personnel benefits as a remedy.

But the justification for grievance-mongering and militancy was hardly as simple as a quest for compensatory gratification. The labor strife of the early 1900s began a tradition in which theories and ideologies could sprout and flourish.

This was the basis of dreams and social utopias, which foresaw the creation of a just and classless society. In certain industrialized countries such as France, sublimating this everyday militancy created a union movement in which grievance-mongering was historically justified as a means of radical societal transformation.

This radical change indeed arrived — with the pervasive impact of the competitive market on economically developed countries. But it did not match the professed utopian vision. Some ventured to call it a crisis of the system. Nevertheless, the shock was so strong that even socialist or communist countries that were in the process of building a new "classless" society were obliged to abandon most of their ideological principles and adopt a realistic attitude.

It is now acknowledged in supposedly classless societies such as the Soviet Union, that the social strata do have divergent interests. It is also acknowledged that the egalitarian trend of the past was due to underdevelopment and not to the radical transformation of society. It is recognized as well that businesses must be profitable and that insolvent businesses must disappear because supporting them artificially deprives efficient companies of needed capital.

In most East European countries, the unions — which enjoy a monopoly — are adopting the language of competition. Their sudden realism is throwing many Western militants off course, but it is comforting to those who long ago adopted a pragmatic attitude after unburdening themselves of social utopias.

This sudden reversal of principles is experienced differently, depending on whether one is a permanent representative of a union group or a wage-earning militant in a plant. For the latter, the historical (utopian) perspective on compensation was motivating, and even stirring, although pragmatism inevitably drives militants to seek new compensations.

Refusal to cooperate with company managers and the rejection of more profitable use of personnel (viewed as exploitation) were typical attitudes of union representatives in the unsaturated market and during the entire high-growth period. But under highly competitive conditions, these same attitudes are likely to stir up ruinous conflicts and even business closures.

It is, however, difficult to change roles and adopt new attitudes. Such actions require learning new skills and often generate fear and the resistance to change, as illustrated in the instance of Raymond Dupont's machine shop.

An upper-management level that draws its prestige from resolving short-term problems will relinquish that role reluctantly and will be hard-pressed to reason on the basis of long-term criteria. A high-level manager accustomed to making minor decisions that have been accorded enhanced importance — because responsibilities are not grouped at the level where most problems arise — will feel wronged if that "right" is taken away. He will have difficulty if given other larger but less "prestigious" tasks as a replacement.

The various roles performed in the old structure are theoretically justified, not only by the unions but also by company managers. Thus, the existence of a large corporate hierarchy within the framework of a rigid organization was only natural, and labor conflicts were a normal occurrence. Acknowledging that these principles are temporary rather than absolute often requires a complete rethinking of the purposes of the organization for all those who sought compensation in hierarchical ambition. It is a difficult adaptation to make.

The competitive market, which imposes profound change, often causes a company's management and labor representation to face the same evolutionary problem. The labor representatives' problem is more dramatic because of their ideological commitment. Despite that obstacle, however, a change of attitude appears inevitable.

It is often accelerated by the presence of strong managers like Raymond Dupont. He succeeded in creating a situation in which the employees no longer experience feelings of frustration but instead can devote themselves to a variety of motivating tasks that require them to utilize their potential and abilities.

Faced with such restructuring, labor representatives must choose between the decline of unionism and a change in their roles. More and more often, they are opting for a radical change in their old roles. Whereas, in the past, they were integrated into the mechanisms of a remedial organization, they can now develop their creative individualism on the job and in their role as representatives, instead of seeking ideological compensation.

There are now instances of labor representatives polling the membership and not distorting the outcome through the application of an outdated evaluation code. They also contribute to creating flexible scheduling, which enables human resources and equipment to be used efficiently. And they support and ensure mobility, not only within the teams but also between work areas and even between different facilities. In addition, they acknowledge that remuneration cannot be guaranteed in the abstract, but must depend on productivity and fluctuations in the competitive market. Finally, in exceptional cases, they accept the fact that certain labor "gains" that have become part of labor law cannot be applied strictly and systematically under new economic circumstances.

Should these roles develop further, labor representation will advantageously fulfill the function of supervision and coordination in companies, so that each person can work according to his skills and abilities.

Will these roles also develop in union groups? Possibly, but progress in that area will surely be long and painful.

An Approach to Organizing Motivation
(see Figure 4, quadrants 11, 12, 13)

When the behavior of top managers is conditioned to a lesser degree than it was in Raymond Dupont's plant, and when there are fewer extreme attitudes, a company can successfully adjust its operational structure rapidly to the new constraints of a competitive market.

Within two years, most work areas can be involved. Even in large firms, where resistance to change is highly structured, significant results can be achieved in a few years. Very successful and concrete examples are proving that fact.

As we have seen, the adaptation process can be accelerated by management to control outcomes and guide the evolution.

Proof of this has been shown many times during the past two decades. Each company must adapt to new competitive circumstances according to its own particular characteristics.

The government is powerless in this arena. At best, it can persuade firms to initiate this difficult change by granting them opportunities for investment financing. However, flexible organizational structure in departments and production units is not created by statutory declaration.

The same is true in all systems of government, even those claiming to have created a classless society. Adaptation of a company's operations to market imperatives depends not on ideology (regardless of its sensibilities) but on principles of social and economic organization. These principles either use or stifle employees' creative individualism, depending on their nature and the requirements of the market.

Human behavior adapts on its own to social and organizational constraints and, as a result, it may turn negative. Then, even in the event of profound change, collective attitudes may lag considerably. Behavior can become stuck in an earlier phase by a multitude of habits, attitudes, principles of reasoning, social values, and emotional reactions.

Such entrenchment in the past is also observed in political, social, and professional areas, but with significant individual variations. Some people quickly abandon their attitude and thinking when the socioeconomic context changes. Others are able to do so only slowly or not at all. The relative nature of such entrenchment lends particular importance to flexible, strong-willed employees, especially during periods of change. They project themselves into the future and plunge into experiments and innovations of all kinds.

For this reason, a company never starts from zero. Even in difficult situations, it is possible to find employees who already have a solution. Quite often, outside consultants search them out because they know that, without them, it would be difficult to set in motion rapid change in departments and production units.

These problem solvers can be found and their contribution can be integrated into a plan for change through the development of a consistent strategy consisting of several stages:

1. Market Demands

Market demands are not uniform. They vary according to business sector, product, and rapidity of technological change.

In the case of Raymond Dupont's plant, the notable market demands included adapting the product to special customer requirements (customizing), continuously improving products (innovation), ensuring impeccable quality, and eliminating unproductive costs (to permit competitive prices).

2. Dysfunctions in the Organization of Work

However, technical, market, and financial requirements are largely inconsistent with the old principle of specialization of jobs and functions. The mechanisms of that principle respond to the imperatives of an unsaturated market, such as stability and uniformity of work.

Listing competitive requirements, identifying dysfunctions in departments and production units, and then measuring the discrepancy between them are important diagnostic tasks. In fact, such discrepancies help identify obstacles blocking developmental change in the operational structure.

3. Market Disturbances

In cases where substantial discrepancies occur, there will also be many "disturbances" — i.e., technical and market demands that the organization of work cannot effectively meet. Analysis and classification of such disturbances by category can yield a better understanding of the source of such obstacles.

4. Different Sources of Obstacles

Obstacles — which generally turn into blockages — indicate the existence of a certain degree of antagonism between market demands and operational mechanisms. Studying their nature and source provides a better understanding of dysfunctions.

Such obstacles usually result from:

- The intensive specialization of jobs and functions
- Traditional distribution of operational, management, and labor relations authority and responsibility

- The inadequacy of various organizational factors and personnel management methods
- Individual and group behavioral conditioning.

If the number of blockages is high, the employees' individualism will be negative and their motivation will be external — i.e., dictated by constraints. Blockages stifle local experimentation and interfere with promising endeavors.

5. Dealing with Obstacles

Recognizing and identifying various obstacles may lead to questions about how to deal with them. Blockages cause significant behavioral reactions at all levels. Analyzing the actors allows us to list and classify such reactions; knowing them facilitates formulating a strategy for action.

The measures used to eliminate obstacles (the most rigid of which turn into blockages) have a variety of effects, depending on whether or not the measure suits the nature of the obstacle. If it is inappropriate, the obstacles may be

- Exacerbated (in the event of "resolution" by conflict, for example)
- Removed one by one (when making adjustments on a case-by-case basis)
- Handled remedially (if specialized levels of management assume responsibility for the disturbances)
- Resolved according to the logic of the old rigid organization (for example, by creating special bonuses or new specialized jobs)
- Circumvented (through costly ad hoc methods).

6. Attitude and Behavior

There is a close correlation between these different measures (for handling obstacles) and individual and group attitudes and behavior.

The one-by-one approach is customarily related to an atmosphere of emotion and conflict. The remedial approach is usually the result of avoidance and defensiveness behavior. In contrast, removal of the obstacles, even partially, is the result of an experimental attitude and actions. The manner of handling obstacles and its effect on individual and group behavior are therefore mutually reinforcing.

7. Identifying the Anchoring Points

Analyzing blockages and obstacles also makes it possible to discover "illegal" or unknown experiments, unanalyzed good results, good ideas put into practice without authorization, etc.

Although blockages and obstacles reveal above all the weak points of the operational structure, discovery of the anchoring points, on the other hand, often indicates the existence of a veritable network of scattered, unknown experiments. They are the enclaves that test effective organizational mechanisms (as in Raymond Dupont's case) and make it possible to motivate employees and unleash their creative individualism. As a result, they respond to the demands of the competitive situation.

8. Unblocking Jobs

In the new economic environment, formulating a good business strategy is not enough to ensure success. If the organization does not lend its full support, plans are likely to be ineffective. Plans can result in either a negative trend, with an accumulation of innumerable small losses, or a positive trend, representing an intensive concentration of efforts within ranks of employees.

The nature of that trend depends on many factors, among which jobs are fundamentally important. Outmoded constraints block the use of creative individualism and generate a negative behavioral trend.

By relying on local experiments and anchoring points, one can undertake a course of action to remove demotivating constraints gradually. That task requires revising the principles of job creation, various personnel management methods, and the distribution of the various powers and responsibilities.

9. Transferring Practical Authority and Responsibility to the Front Lines of the Organization

The transfer of management and operational authority and responsibility is presently facilitated by rapid technological development, which no longer requires a forceful and overbearing managerial staff as in the past, nor a highly specialized compartmentalization of the work process.

Nevertheless, such a transfer often meets considerable resistance to change because such responsibilities traditionally represent a source of prestige and power. As a result, the transfer must be done locally and gradually, relying on anchoring points.

What is the advantage of such a reform? The management will be relieved of short-term problem solving and it can then address long-term planning and business strategy. Units, departments, and production units will thus set their own practical goals for reaching specified targets, which is much more motivating than carrying out orders from higher up.

10. New Operational Mechanisms

Eliminating outmoded constraints and, at the same time, transferring practical powers and authority to lower levels of the organization requires the implementation of new operational mechanisms. This should be done experimentally (as in Dupont's supervisor group) by continually relying on the results of small successful experiments.

Such mechanisms are based on participation, the assumption of responsibility, and motivation. They render leadership authority, in the traditional sense of the term, unnecessary.

11. *Universal Application of the Principle of Creative Individualism*

The replication of a successful program can be rapid, but it must be gradual. It usually takes place on two planes — organizational and behavioral.

A now long-standing discussion contrasts two approaches in that regard. Some theories claim that any significant change within a company presupposes a structural and organizational reform. Other theories stress that individual and group behavior must change first, and reforms come only later.

Raymond Dupont's experiment and the profound transformation of his work area illustrate that the two approaches are complementary; they must be applied together in the context of a developmental strategy.

In the case of Dupont's team, which was embedded in a rigid organization, an official or negotiated elimination of the individual output system could not be expected. For that reason, Dupont had to gamble specifically on his workers' expectations and understanding. In relying on their favorable attitude, however, he succeeded in carrying out an organizational reform — i.e., the implementation of the collective output system.

In subsequent phases of that course of action, the organizational situation was unblocked. Successive reforms included expanded implementation of skill groups, formation of the supervisor group, elimination of two levels of management, and transfer of certain practical authority and responsibility to lower levels of the organization.

If the organizational and behavioral components of the course of action undertaken overlap harmoniously, and if the last vestiges of resistance to change are successfully eliminated, then the development of an individualized organization can culminate in the practice of skill-based competition.

Postscript

For many decades, Raymond Dupont has seen various flags, theories, and ideologies march into the social and political arena but never interfere with what, for him, is essential. That essential element is his participation in his country's business sector and the use of his skills and abilities in his job.

The number of middlemen between him and the responsibilities he *could* assume is still large — elected officials (who have become professional politicians), labor representatives (who turn their aspirations into grievance-mongering), superiors within the corporate hierarchy (who assume responsibility for resolving front-line problems), administrative middlemen (who process his work in their own way), and labor mediators (who negotiate with the unions to resolve his problems instead of discussing them with him).

Can he play a role that uses his intelligence, abilities, and motivation in the interest of his employer and society?

Ultimately, as soon as his skills are summoned forth and he can promote his potential and abilities, his creative individualism can operate successfully within the framework of an individualized organization.

The highly competitive market requires initiative at all levels. Today the individual abilities of employees are the driving force of economic growth. And those who work in organizations based on the principle of creative individualism constructively place their abilities and skills in the service of that economic growth.

About the Author

Étienne Minarik was born in Budapest, Hungary. A student of literature and economics, he majored in pedagogy and taught educational methods to junior high school teachers in Budapest from 1951 to 1956. He emigrated from Hungary in 1957 after deep involvement in the uprising of 1957. He has lived in France since 1958.

After working for several years in a factory in France, Mr. Minarik returned to college and earned degrees in psychology and the sociology of work. From 1968 to 1971 he was a management consultant in a large automobile firm. In collaboration with the French institute *Entreprise et Personnel*, he subsequently consulted on work organization and human relations for a number of leading French companies, including Rhône-Poulenc, Renault, SNR, Seita, and SNEAP.

Mr. Minarik has also taught work sociology at the Institute of Politics, Strasbourg, and at the High School for Engineers in Lyons. He is the author of many journal articles and two previous books on psychosociology and work skills.

Index

BOOKS AVAILABLE FROM PRODUCTIVITY PRESS

Productivity Press publishes and distributes materials on continuous improvement in productivity, quality, customer service, and the creative involvement of all employees. Many of our products are direct source materials from Japan that have been translated into English for the first time and are available exclusively from Productivity. Supplemental products and services include newsletters, conferences, seminars, in-house training and consulting, audio-visual training programs, and industrial study missions. Call 1-800-274-9911 for our free bookcatalog.

CEDAC
A Tool for Continuous Systematic Improvement
Ryuji Fukuda

CEDAC, or Cause and Effect Diagram with the Addition of Cards, is a modification of the "fishbone diagram," one of the standard QC tools. One of the most powerful, yet simple problem-solving methods to come out of Japan (Fukuda won a Deming Prize for developing it), CEDAC actually encompasses a whole cluster of tools for continuous systematic improvement. They include window analysis (for identifying problems), the CEDAC diagram (for analyzing problems and developing standards), and window development (for ensuring adherence to standards). Here is Fukuda's manual for the in-house support of improvement activities using CEDAC. It provides step by step directions for setting up and using CEDAC. With a text that's concise, clear, and to the point, nearly 50 illustrations and sample forms suitable for transparencies, and a removable CEDAC wall chart, the manual is an ideal training aid.
ISBN 0-915299-26-7 / 144 pages / $49.95 / Order code CEDAC-B200

The Visual Factory
Building Participation Through Shared Information
Michel Greif

If you're aware of the tremendous improvements achieved in productivity and quality as a result of employee involvement, then you'll appreciate the great value of creating a visual factory. This book shows how visual management can be used to make the factory a place where workers and supervisors freely communicate and take improvement action. It details how to develop meeting and communication areas, communicate work standards and instructions, use visual production controls such as kanban, and make goals and progress visible. Over 200 diagrams and photos illustrate the numerous visual techniques discussed.
ISBN 0-915299-67-4 / 320 pages / $49.95 / Order code VFAC-B200

Manager Revolution!
A Guide to Survival in Today's Changing Workplace
Yoshio Hatakeyama

An extraordinary blueprint for effective management, here is a step-by-step guide to improving your skills, both in everyday performance and in long-term planning. *Manager Revolution!* explores in detail the basics of the Japanese success story and proves that it is readily transferable to other settings. Written by the president of the Japan Management Association and a bestseller in Japan, here is a survival kit for beginning and seasoned managers alike. Each chapter includes case studies, checklists, and self-tests.

ISBN 0-915299-10-0 / 208 pages / $24.95 / MREV-B200

Kaizen Teian 1
Developing Systems for Continuous Improvement
Through Employee Suggestions
Japan Human Relations Association (ed.)

Especially relevant for middle and upper managers, this book focuses on the role of managers as catalysts in spurring employee ideas and facilitating their implementation. It explains how to run a proposal program on a day-to-day basis, outlines the policies that support a "bottom-up" system of innovation, and defines the three main objectives of kaizen teian: to build participation, develop individual skills, and achieve higher profits.

ISBN 0-915299-89-5 / 208 pages /$39.93 / Order code KT1-BK

The Idea Book
Improvement Through Total Employee Involvement
Japan Human Relations Association (ed.)

What would your company be like if each employee — from line workers to engineers to sales people — gave 100 ideas every year for improving the company? This handbook of Japanese-style suggestion systems (called "teian"), will help your company develop its own vital improvement system by getting all employees involved. Train workers how to write improvement proposals, help supervisors promote participation, and put creative problem solving to work in your company. Designed as a self-trainer and study group tool, the book is heavily illustrated and includes hundreds of examples. (Spanish edition available.)

ISBN 0-915299-22-4 / 240 pages / $49.95 / Order code IDEA-B200

Productivity Press, Inc., Dept. BK, P.O. Box 3007, Cambridge, MA 02140 1-800-274-9911

The Best of TEI
Current Perspectives on Total Employee Involvement
Karen Jones (ed.)

An outstanding compilation of the 29 best presentations from the first three International Total Employee Involvement (TEI) conferences sponsored by Productivity. You'll find sections on management strategy, case studies, training and retraining, kaizen (continuous improvement), and high quality teamwork. Here's the cutting edge in implemented EI strategies doubly valuable to you because it comprises both theory and practice. It's also amply illustrated with presentation charts. Whether you're a manager, a team member, or in HR development, you'll find The Best of TEI a rich and stimulating source of information. Comes in handy 3-ring binder.
ISBN 0-915299-63-1 / 502 pages / $175.00 / Order code TEI-B200

Caught in the Middle
A Leadership Guide for Partnership in the Workplace
Rick Maurer

Many of today's supervisors and middle managers have received a mandate to "get employees involved" in their workplace. The challenge is to initiate participation, maximize its effects, and keep involvement high on a daily basis. This lively, easily-read book provides the inspiration and know-how to achieve these goals as it brings to light the rewards of establishing a partnership with your staff.
ISBN 1-56327-004-8 / 144 pages / $24.95 / Order code CAUGHT-B200

The Improvement Book
Creating the Problem-Free Workplace
Tomo Sugiyama

A practical guide to setting up a participatory problem-solving system in the workplace. Focusing on ways to eliminate the "Big 3" problems irrationality, inconsistency, and waste this book provides clear direction for starting a "problem-free engineering" program. It also gives you a full introduction to basic concepts of industrial housekeeping (known in Japan as 5S), two chapters of examples that can be used in small group training activities, and a workbook for individual use (extra copies are available separately). Written in an informal style, and using many anecdotes and examples, this book provides a proven approach to problem solving for any industrial setting.
ISBN 0-915299-47-X / 236 pages / $49.95 / Order code IB-B200

40 Years, 20 Million Ideas
The Toyota Suggestion System
Yuzo Yasuda

This fascinating book describes how Toyota generated tremendous employee involvement in their creative idea suggestion system. It reviews the program's origins, Toyota's internal promotion of the system, and examples of actual suggestions and how they were used. This account reveals the role of the Good Idea Club an autonomous, in-house organization begun by gold-prize award winners, in fostering suggestion-writing ability. Personal accounts and anecdotes flavor the text, address problems encountered and their resolutions, and convey how trust and understanding became key elements of employee/management relationships at Toyota. This case study will give any reader the inspiration to initiate a creative idea suggestion system of their own or significantly revitalize an existing one.

ISBN 0-915299-74-7 / 224 pages / $39.95 / Order code 4020-B200

Better Makes Us Best

Dr. John Psarouthakis

A short, engaging, but powerful and highly practical guide to performance improvement for any business or individual. Focusing on incremental progress toward clear goals is the key you become "better" day by day. It's a realistic, personally fulfilling, action-oriented, and dynamic philosophy that has made Psarouthakis's own company a member of the Fortune 500 in just ten years. Buy a copy for everyone in your work force, and let it work for you.

ISBN 0-915299-56-9 / 112 pages / $16.95 / Order code BMUB-B200

TEI NEWSLETTER

TEI — Total Employee Involvement — can transform an unproductive, inefficient, even angry work force into a smart, productive, cooperative team. Learn how by reading the monthly TEI . Its articles, interviews, suggestions, and case histories will help you promote a learning organization, activate continuous improvement, and encourage creativity in all your employees. To subscribe, or for more information, call 1-800-899-5009. Please state order code "BA200" when ordering.

COMPLETE LIST OF TITLES FROM PRODUCTIVITY PRESS

Akao, Yoji (ed.). **Quality Function Deployment: Integrating Customer Requirements into Product Design**
ISBN 0-915299-41-0 / 1990 / 387 pages / $ 75.00 / order code QFD

Akiyama, Kaneo. **Function Analysis: Systematic Improvement of Quality and Performance**
ISBN 0-915299-81-X / 1991 / 288 pages / $59.95 / order code FA

Asaka, Tetsuichi and Kazuo Ozeki (eds.). **Handbook of Quality Tools: The Japanese Approach**
ISBN 0-915299-45-3 / 1990 / 336 pages / $59.95 / order code HQT

Belohlav, James A. **Championship Management: An Action Model for High Performance**
ISBN 0-915299-76-3 / 1990 / 265 pages / $29.95 / order code CHAMPS

Birkholz, Charles and Jim Villella. **The Battle to Stay Competitive: Changing the Traditional Workplace**
ISBN 0-915299-96-8 / 1991 / 110 pages paper / $9.95 /order code BATTLE

Christopher, William F. **Productivity Measurement Handbook**
ISBN 0-915299-05-4 / 1985 / 680 pages / $137.95 / order code PMH

D'Egidio, Franco. **The Service Era: Leadership in a Global Environment**
ISBN 0-915299-68-2 / 1990 / 165 pages / $29.95 / order code SERA

Ford, Henry. **Today and Tomorrow**
ISBN 0-915299-36-4 / 1988 / 286 pages / $24.95 / order code FORD

Fukuda, Ryuji. **CEDAC: A Tool for Continuous Systematic Improvement**
ISBN 0-915299-26-7 / 1990 / 144 pages / $49.95 / order code CEDAC

Fukuda, Ryuji. **Managerial Engineering: Techniques for Improving Quality and Productivity in the Workplace** (rev.)
ISBN 0-915299-09-7 / 1986 / 208 pages / $39.95 / order code ME

Gotoh, Fumio. **Equipment Planning for TPM: Maintenance Prevention Design**
ISBN 0-915299-77-1 / 1991 / 320 pages / $75.00 / order code ETPM

Greif, Michel. **The Visual Factory: Building Participation Through Shared Information**
ISBN 0-915299-67-4 / 1991 / 320 pages / $49.95 / order code VFAC

Hatakeyama, Yoshio. **Manager Revolution! A Guide to Survival in Today's Changing Workplace**
ISBN 0-915299-10-0 / 1986 / 208 pages / $24.95 / order code MREV

Hirano, Hiroyuki. **JIT Factory Revolution: A Pictorial Guide to Factory Design of the Future**
ISBN 0-915299-44-5 / 1989 / 227 pages / $49.95 / order code JITFAC

Hirano, Hiroyuki. **JIT Implementation Manual: The Complete Guide to Just-In-Time Manufacturing**
ISBN 0-915299-66-6 / 1990 / 1006 pages / $2500.00 / order code HIRJIT

Horovitz, Jacques. **Winning Ways: Achieving Zero-Defect Service**
ISBN 0-915299-78-X / 1990 / 165 pages / $24.95 / order code WWAYS

Ishiwata, Junichi. **IE for the Shop Floor: Productivity Through Process Analysis**
ISBN 0-915299-82-8 / 1991 / 208 pages / $39.95 / order code SHOPF1

Productivity Press, Inc., Dept. BK, P.O. Box 3007, Cambridge, MA 02140 1-800-274-9911

Japan Human Relations Association (ed.). **The Idea Book: Improvement Through TEI (Total Employee Involvement)**
ISBN 0-915299-22-4 / 1988 / 232 pages / $49.95 / order code IDEA

Japan Human Relations Association (ed.). **The Service Industry Idea Book: Employee Involvement in Retail and Office Improvement**
ISBN 0-915299-65-8 / 1991 / 294 pages / $49.95 / order code SIDEA

Japan Management Association (ed.). **Kanban and Just-In-Time at Toyota: Management Begins at the Workplace** (rev.), Translated by David J. Lu
ISBN 0-915299-48-8 / 1989 / 224 pages / $36.50 / order code KAN

Japan Management Association and Constance E. Dyer. **The Canon Production System: Creative Involvement of the Total Workforce**
ISBN 0-915299-06-2 / 1987 / 251 pages / $36.95 / order code CAN

Jones, Karen (ed.). **The Best of TEI: Current Perspectives on Total Employee Involvement**
ISBN 0-915299-63-1 / 1989 / 502 pages / $175.00 / order code TEI

JUSE. **TQC Solutions: The 14-Step Process**
ISBN 0-915299-79-8 / 1991 / 416 pages / 2 volumes / $120.00 / order code TQCS

Kanatsu, Takashi. **TQC for Accounting: A New Role in Companywide Improvement**
ISBN 0-915299-73-9 / 1991 / 244 pages / $45.00 / order code TQCA

Karatsu, Hajime. **Tough Words For American Industry**
ISBN 0-915299-25-9 / 1988 / 178 pages / $24.95 / order code TOUGH

Karatsu, Hajime. **TQC Wisdom of Japan: Managing for Total Quality Control**, Translated by David J. Lu
ISBN 0-915299-18-6 / 1988 / 136 pages / $34.95 / order code WISD

Kato, Kenichiro. **I.E. for the Shop Floor: Productivity Through Motion Study**
ISBN 1-56327-000-5 / 1991 / 224 pages / $39.95 / order code SHOPF2

Kaydos, Will. **Measuring, Managing, and Maximizing Performance**
ISBN 0-915299- 98-4 / 1991 / 304 pages / $34.95 / order code MMMP

Kobayashi, Iwao. **20 Keys to Workplace Improvement**
ISBN 0-915299-61-5 / 1990 / 264 pages / $34.95 / order code 20KEYS

Lu, David J. **Inside Corporate Japan: The Art of Fumble-Free Management**
ISBN 0-915299-16-X / 1987 / 278 pages / $24.95 / order code ICJ

Maskell, Brian H. **Performance Measurement for World Class Manufacturing: A Model for American Companies**
ISBN 0-915299-99-2 / 1991 / 448 pages / $49.95 / order code PERFM

Merli, Giorgio. **Co-makership: The New Supply Strategy for Manufacturers**
ISBN 0915299-84-4 / 1991 / 224 pages / $39.95 / order code COMAKE

Merli, Giorgio. **Total Manufacturing Management: Production Organization for the 1990s**
ISBN 0-915299-58-5 / 1990 / 224 pages / $39.95 / order code TMM

Mizuno, Shigeru (ed.). **Management for Quality Improvement: The 7 New QC Tools**
ISBN 0-915299-29-1 / 1988 / 324 pages / $59.95 / order code 7QC

Monden, Yasuhiro and Michiharu Sakurai (eds.). **Japanese Management Accounting: A World Class Approach to Profit Management**
ISBN 0-915299-50-X / 1990 / 568 pages / $59.95 / order code JMACT

Productivity Press, Inc., Dept. BK, P.O. Box 3007, Cambridge, MA 02140 1-800-274-9911

Nachi-Fujikoshi (ed.). **Training for TPM: A Manufacturing Success Story**
ISBN 0-915299-34-8 / 1990 / 272 pages / $59.95 / order code CTPM

Nakajima, Seiichi. **Introduction to TPM: Total Productive Maintenance**
ISBN 0-915299-23-2 / 1988 / 149 pages / $45.00 / order code ITPM

Nakajima, Seiichi. **TPM Development Program: Implementing Total Productive Maintenance**
ISBN 0-915299-37-2 / 1989 / 428 pages / $85.00 / order code DTPM

Nikkan Kogyo Shimbun, Ltd./Factory Magazine (ed.). **Poka-yoke: Improving Product Quality by Preventing Defects**
ISBN 0-915299-31-3 / 1989 / 288 pages / $59.95 / order code IPOKA

Nikkan Kogyo Shimbun/Esme McTighe (ed.). **Factory Management Notebook Series: Mixed Model Production**
ISBN 0-915299-97-6 / 1991 / 184 / $125.00 / order code N1-MM

Nikkan Kogyo Shimbun/Esme McTighe (ed.). **Factory Management Notebook Series: Visual Control Systems**
ISBN 0-915299-54-2 / 1991 / 194 pages / $125.00 / order code N1-VCS

Nikkan Kogyo Shimbun/Esme McTighe (ed.). **Factory Management Notebook Series: Autonomation/Automation**
ISBN 0-0-56327-002-1 / 1991 / 200 pages / $125.00 / order code N1-AA

Ohno, Taiichi. **Toyota Production System: Beyond Large-Scale Production**
ISBN 0-915299-14-3 / 1988 / 162 pages / $39.95 / order code OTPS

Ohno, Taiichi. **Workplace Management**
ISBN 0-915299-19-4 / 1988 / 165 pages / $34.95 / order code WPM

Ohno, Taiichi and Setsuo Mito. **Just-In-Time for Today and Tomorrow**
ISBN 0-915299-20-8 / 1988 / 208 pages / $34.95 / order code OMJIT

Perigord, Michel. **Achieving Total Quality Management: A Program for Action**
ISBN 0-915299-60-7 / 1991 / 384 pages / $45.00 / order code ACHTQM

Psarouthakis, John. **Better Makes Us Best**
ISBN 0-915299-56-9 / 1989 / 112 pages / $16.95 / order code BMUB

Robinson, Alan. **Continuous Improvement in Operations: A Systematic Approach to Waste Reduction**
ISBN 0-915299-51-8 / 1991 / 416 pages / $34.95 / order code ROB2-C

Robson, Ross (ed.). **The Quality and Productivity Equation: American Corporate Strategies for the 1990s**
ISBN 0-915299-71-2 / 1990 / 558 pages / $29.95 / order code QPE

Shetty, Y.K and Vernon M. Buehler (eds.). **Competing Through Productivity and Quality**
ISBN 0-915299-43-7 / 1989 / 576 pages / $39.95 / order code COMP

Shingo, Shigeo. **Non-Stock Production: The Shingo System for Continuous Improvement**
ISBN 0-915299-30-5 / 1988 / 480 pages / $75.00 / order code NON

Shingo, Shigeo. **A Revolution In Manufacturing: The SMED System**, Translated by Andrew P. Dillon
ISBN 0-915299-03-8 / 1985 / 383 pages / $70.00 / order code SMED

Shingo, Shigeo. **The Sayings of Shigeo Shingo: Key Strategies for Plant Improvement**, Translated by Andrew P. Dillon
ISBN 0-915299-15-1 / 1987 / 208 pages / $39.95 / order code SAY

Productivity Press, Inc., Dept. BK, P.O. Box 3007, Cambridge, MA 02140 1-800-274-9911

Shingo, Shigeo. **A Study of the Toyota Production System from an Industrial Engineering Viewpoint**
ISBN 0-915299-17-8 / 1989 / 293 pages / $39.95 / order code STREV

Shingo, Shigeo. **Zero Quality Control: Source Inspection and the Poka-yoke System**, Translated by Andrew P. Dillon
ISBN 0-915299-07-0 / 1986 / 328 pages / $70.00 / order code ZQC

Shinohara, Isao (ed.). **New Production System: JIT Crossing Industry Boundaries**
ISBN 0-915299-21-6 / 1988 / 224 pages / $34.95 / order code NPS

Sugiyama, Tomo. **The Improvement Book: Creating the Problem-Free Workplace**
ISBN 0-915299-47-X / 1989 / 236 pages / $49.95 / order code IB

Suzue, Toshio and Akira Kohdate. **Variety Reduction Program (VRP): A Production Strategy for Product Diversification**
ISBN 0-915299-32-1 / 1990 / 164 pages / $59.95 / order code VRP

Tateisi, Kazuma. **The Eternal Venture Spirit: An Executive's Practical Philosophy**
ISBN 0-915299-55-0 / 1989 / 208 pages/ $19.95 / order code EVS

Yasuda, Yuzo. **40 Years, 20 Million Ideas: The Toyota Suggestion System**
ISBN 0-915299-74-7 / 1991 / 210 pages / $39.95 / order code 4020

Audio-Visual Programs

Japan Management Association. **Total Productive Maintenance: Maximizing Productivity and Quality**
ISBN 0-915299-46-1 / 167 slides / 1989 / $749.00 / order code STPM
ISBN 0-915299-49-6 / 2 videos / 1989 / $749.00 / order code VTPM

Shingo, Shigeo. **The SMED System**, Translated by Andrew P. Dillon
ISBN 0-915299-11-9 / 181 slides / 1986 / $749.00 / order code S5
ISBN 0-915299-27-5 / 2 videos / 1987 / $749.00 / order code V5

Shingo, Shigeo. **The Poka-yoke System**, Translated by Andrew P. Dillon
ISBN 0-915299-13-5 / 235 slides / 1987 / $749.00 / order code S6
ISBN 0-915299-28-3 / 2 videos / 1987 / $749.00 / order code V6

Returns of AV programs willl be accepted for incorrect or damaged shipments only.

TO ORDER: Write, phone, or fax Productivity Press, Dept. BK, P.O. Box 3007, Cambridge, MA 02140, phone 1-800-274-9911, fax 617-864-6286. Send check or charge to your credit card (American Express, Visa, MasterCard accepted).

U.S. ORDERS: Add $5 shipping for first book, $2 each additional for UPS surface delivery. CT residents add 8% and MA residents 5% sales tax. For each AV program that you order, add $5 for programs with 1 or 2 tapes, and $12 for programs with 3 or more tapes.

INTERNATIONAL ORDERS: Write, phone, or fax for quote and indicate shipping method desired. Pre-payment in U.S. dollars must accompany your order (checks must be drawn on U.S. banks). When quote is returned with payment, your order will be shipped promptly by the method requested.

NOTE: Prices subject to change without notice.

Productivity Press, Inc., Dept. BK, P.O. Box 3007, Cambridge, MA 02140 1-800-274-9911